Dance of the Dialectic

Happy 19th Birthday Don —

Rob (Sol)

Dance of the Dialectic

How Pierre Elliott Trudeau
went from Philosopher-King to
the Incorruptible Robespierre
to Philosopher-Queen
Marie Antoinette to
Canada's Generalissimo Ky
and then to Mackenzie King
and even better.

Larry Zolf

James Lewis & Samuel, Publishers

Parts of this book first appeared in the October 1973 issue of *Saturday Night*.

ISBN 0-88862-053-5 (cloth)
ISBN 0-88862-052-7 (paper)

Designed by Lynn Campbell
Cover by Duncan MacPherson

James Lewis & Samuel, Publishers
35 Britain Street
Toronto 229
Canada

Printed and bound in Canada

Contents

Preface vii

Athens on the Rideau
1. Charisma: Trudeau as "Oscar," the Socratic Academy Award 3
2. The Global Village Idiots 11
3. Punditi-in, Punditi-out and Radical Chicci 15

Post-Charisma: Trudeau and the New National Mood
4. From the Good Old Seven Days to the Brightest and the Best 23
5. Bread on the Waters of the Rideau 31
6. Two Canadas—Diefenbaker's and Trudeau's 35

Storming the Gates of the Lyceum
7. The Revolt of the Peasant Paparazzi 43

The Incredible Alternatives
8. From Forlorn Bob to Robert Lazarus 55
9. Lewis: From David to Goliath and Back Again 63

Messages for the Emperor
10. The Messengers: All Quiet on the Lyceum Front 73
11. Canada First, Trudeau Last 77

Conversations with Canadians
12. The Odd Couple: The Jaded Observer in Happy and Unhappy Colloquy with the Friendly Trudeaucrat 83
13. Message Received: The Folding of the Universe and Lessons Learned 95

Epilogue 111

Glossary 113

This slim little volume of penetrating political insights is dedicated to Robert Fulford, editor of *Saturday Night,* whose modest request for a modest article on the modest Rt. Hon. Pierre Elliott Trudeau resulted in this modest little fraud that I'm now perpetrating on the Canadian public; and to

Lister Sinclair, executive vice-president of the CBC, whose love of originality and creativity first made me (CBC employee, number 437-389-836) think that this project was legally and morally possible.

Preface

I would have loved to have dedicated this book to my wife, who, to quote Dalton Camp, "endured all this, including the re-telling" (not to mention the re-typing) but, since I am a life-long confirmed bachelor, such a dedication seemed to me both trite and redundant.

I *would* like to thank the Bronfman, Labatt and Molson families, whose excellent products sustained me in dark moments and eased the pain of frequent attacks of writer's block.

It pains me to say that this slim little volume is *not* the definitive work on the Parliamentary Press Gallery, the Rt. Hon. Pierre Elliott Trudeau, the Hon. Robert Lorne Stanfield, David Lewis, MP, or, for that matter, Dr. Stanley Haidasz. I was planning a definitive biography of the latter gentleman, a slim book, perhaps ten pages, perhaps more, entitled *Haidasz: The Old Charisma,* by Larry Zolf, the new charisma, but that project failed due to my inexplicable incapacity to obtain copies of the Ostry-Haidasz correspondence.

I'm aware that it's traditional for authors to say that "this book could not have been written without the cooperation and generosity of hundreds of people" (John Meisel, *The Canadian General Election of 1957,* Toronto: University of Toronto Press, 1962, preface, ix). But to hell with tradition. This book was written with the cooperation and generosity of:

George Gagné, clerk of the Parliamentary Press Gallery and custodian of its ancient spirituous sanctuary, who was always there with a drink when I needed it; ditto for Louis at the National Press Club and ditto too to cabinet ministers, MPs and their wives too numerous to mention who provided the needed libations in times of stress with no questions asked. (They also serve who merely stand and wait upon those about to fall.)

This book was also written with the "cooperation and generosity" of Press Gallery colleagues Douglas Fisher of the Toronto *Sun,* Arthur Blakeley, Ottawa correspondent for the Montreal *Gazette,* Victor Mackie, FP Publications, and Gail Scott, CTV News. Mr. Fisher spent many Ottawa hours with me in both good and bad times, talking about politics and politicians in a way I always found enjoyable. Mr. Fisher also paid me the courtesy of respecting what little news judgement and sense of humour I possess. This courtesy was further extended to me by Messrs. Blakeley and Mackie, whose ability to roll about on the floor in fits of laughter at the slightest thing I said never ceased to amaze me. As for Gail Scott, so militant a feminist that she deliberately married Mr. Graham Scott (Mr. Stanfield's executive assistant) so as not to have to change her name, one can only say "thanks" for many kindnesses. In this connection I would also like to thank Marjorie Nichols, who once toiled for the Ottawa *Journal* in the gallery, for showing me the way to the little boys' room on the third floor, Centre Block, House of Commons.

At this point it is only fair to say that this book was written without the cooperation and generosity of:
The Royal Canadian Mounted Police
The Rt. Hon. Pierre Elliott Trudeau
The Rt. Hon. John George Diefenbaker
The Hon. Robert Lorne Stanfield
David Lewis, MP

The Seven Dwarfs
Richard Neilsen
The Jaded Observer
Phat Ferns
The Hunchback of Notre Dame
Terry Hargreaves
The Lone Ranger and Tonto
Dalton Camp
Bernard Ostry
The Maltese Falcon
Cameron Graham
Pinocchio
Laurent Picard
Mrs. Beryl Plumptre and the Food Prices
    Review Board

At this point, too, let me deal with the traditional author's statement: "My only regret is that the number of my creditors is so great they cannot all be mentioned" (John Meisel, *The Canadian General Election of 1957,* Toronto: University of Toronto Press, 1962, preface, ix). Balderdash! My only regret is that the number of my creditors is so small they *can* all be mentioned.

My creditors are:
Victoria and Grey Trust
The Canadian Imperial Bank of Commerce
The Department of National Revenue

So much for clichés. En passant, I suppose, it might perhaps be worthwhile to mention some bibliographical stimuli that gave me an occasional rise. Top places on my bibliographic list would have to go to the Ottawa-Hull and Toronto telephone directories. Many, perhaps all, of the names found in those two volumes have been dropped by me into this small volume. Occasionally, the intrepid readers of this shrivelled opus will stumble across titles of books and names of authors. I have never read these books, nor met these authors. I *have* read *Winnie the Pooh* and the one time I did meet A.A. Milne I found her to be a distinguished, kind and courteous lady (person).

Finally, some acknowledgements. I would like to thank Mr. James Davey, former program secretary to the prime minister and now special adviser to the minister of Transport; Mr. Allan Gotlieb, deputy minister of Manpower and Immigration; Professors John Munro and Alex Inglis, editors of *The Memoirs of the Right Honourable Lester B. Pearson;* Gerry Yanover, special assistant to the Hon. Allan MacEachen; William Grogan, special assistant to the Hon. Robert Lorne Stanfield; and Douglas Fisher, for reading this book in its manuscript form. Their comments, responses, praises and criticisms are not fit to print.

In closing, I would like to disabuse anyone of the notion that I take full responsibility for all opinions, insights, banalities and sheer prattle contained in these pages and those to follow.

Full responsibility for all opinions, insights, banalities and sheer prattle contained in these pages and those to follow falls upon the exclusive shoulders of my solicitor, Hart Pomerantz:

Pomerantz & Pearl
Barristers and Solicitors
27 Prince Arthur Street
Toronto 180, Ontario
This Is The Law, Hart, and don't you forget it!

And now, here's Larry, Pierre, Robert, John, David, etc., etc., etc.

Athens on the Rideau

Chapter One
Charisma:
Trudeau as "Oscar,"
the Socratic Academy Award

As I watched the daily manoeuvrings, posturings, pratfalls and tours de force of the fragile 29th Parliament during the first half of 1973, my mind frequently drifted back—as it so often does—to childhood days in Winnipeg. Sometime in the early forties, while bouncing on my father's knee, I heard one Leibel Basman, the Bolshevik philosopher-king of our neighbourhood, inform my father (Mr. Basman's best friend as well as his bitterest political opponent) that one Karl Marx had stood one Friedrich Hegel on his head. At that tender age I took this observation to mean that Mr. Marx and Mr. Hegel were just one more carnival act I could look forward to seeing at the Conklin Brothers or the Royal American Shows that visited Winnipeg each summer.

Years later, while attending Winnipeg's United College, dear alma mater to the likes of J.S. Woodsworth (Canada's official political saint), Stanley Knowles (now serving his tenth term in the House of Commons) and Harry Backlin (a college classmate and friend of mine who served one term at Stony Mountain penitentiary for a gold robbery in 1966), I at last learned the true meaning of Mr. Basman's famous one-liner. It seems Mr. Hegel believed that ideas ultimately shaped the social, economic and political condition of man, while Mr. Marx perversely believed that social, economic and political realities shaped the ideas of man.

Now, you may ask, what have philosopher-kings, Messrs. Marx and Hegel and standing on one's head to do with the understanding of Ottawa's current political climate? Perhaps nothing, but they provide this reporter with one useful tool for making some sense of the stuff and nonsense of Ottawa's contemporary political scene.

For one thing, philosopher-kings, Messrs. Marx and Hegel and standing on one's head certainly bring to mind the Rt. Hon. Pierre Elliott Trudeau. In the late sixties it was a well-known fact that Mr. Trudeau was a devout practitioner of Yoga. As part of that system's demanding regimen, he frequently stood on his head. The process, I'm told, relaxes the limbs and torso and brings the blood rushing to the brain. As a consequence, one achieves tranquillity, a sense of inner purpose and a clue to the meaning of life. What Mr. Trudeau learned standing on his head seemed to reinforce the lessons learnt as world traveller and scholar-critic-activist in the Quebec of the 1950s. As a philosopher, Mr. Trudeau was a Hegelian; in 1968, as the new prime minister, more anointed than elected by the Canadian people, Mr. Trudeau was a philosopher-king.

Indeed, the Trudeau career itself was walking and living proof that ideas ultimately shaped socio-economic and political realities. *Cité Libre* did its part in the final destruction of the venal materialism of the Duplessis system. The Absolute-ism of One Canada and the majority government it brought in its wake put an end to five years of Pearsonian piecemeal social engineering.

Henceforth there would be an end to the Munichian appeasement of French-Canadian nationalism. The superstructure of Canadian federalism would once again be restored to its proper place in the universe, unfolding as it should, rather than caving in to the ego-tripping whims of Quebec bourgeois nationalists. Trudeau brick and mortar were to replace Pearsonian straws in the wind.

With the superstructure safely in place, the structure of Canadian society itself could be tackled and tamed. To Trudeau and his fellow Idea-men, the Canadian political scene had for far too long been the exclusive preserve of the sentimentalists and the necromancers. Instead of National Dreaming there would now be a firm grip on reality; instead of crystal balls—real balls.

For what Trudeau promised was not only a Canada, One and Indivisible, but a Canadian society, truly Just. From the very battlements of Parliament Hill, the new credo of the Just Society rang loud and clear: to each according to his needs, from each according to his ability. And ability was the one thing the Trudeau forces were supposed to have in abundance. For, as Plato put it, the foundation of the Just Society was the Just Man and the Just Man was he who did his own thing, "the thing to which his nature was best adapted." The Trudeau thing was the ability to govern, "to fix one's eye upon immutable principles and to fashion States after the heavenly image."

And thus, in the four years of Trudeau majority government, Parliament Hill was converted into a miniature Athens. The hapless opposition parties, floundering in the Cave of Darkness, watching the shadows of the Just Society flickering by, were the dromedaries, the slaves and the "nobodies" in the new scheme of things. The Liberal backbenchers became the Men of Brass, the plebians and potential cannon fodder of the Just Society. Messrs. Marchand, Pelletier, Pepin, Turner, Benson et al, became the Just Society's warrior class and, ready or not, were to defend the new system with their very lives.

As for the Privy Council Office and the Prime Minister's Office, why that was the very Lyceum itself! There the immutables and inscrutables were immersed into think-tanks whose critical path flows were in perpetual motion. There the shocks of Futurism were to be painlessly and systematically removed. There the time-frame for decision-making numbered not in days and years, but in decades.

And from the East Block Lyceum the Ideas poured forth. Here the Dance of the Dialectic was a marathon affair. Each day the Thesis trotted forth to do one more tango with the Antithesis, as a breathless nation watched and waited in the stands for a final solution.

Thus in the famous Battle of Wounded Groin Canadians watched their native peoples say No to a White Paper that offered to replace the empty fleshpots of the reserve with the equally empty melting pot of the urban Canadian mosaic. The crowd cheered as the Lyceum pronounced that, henceforth, the poor would not always be with us.

Tax Reform and the Family Income Security Plan would force the greedy to help the needy. The rich would pay their capital gains tax and so would the family farmer and the small businessman. The rich would not get their family allowance cheques and neither would the big city breadwinner making $10,500 a year. The Department of Regional Economic Expansion would persuade American business to open branchplants in the Maritimes and Quebec to replace the ones they'd just shut down in Ontario. Pensioners, widows, orphans and exports would be protected by the War Against Inflation. The dangers of radioactive economic fallout would be contained by the umbrella of a new unemployment insurance scheme.

Should that not suffice, then labour-intensive manufacturing and processing industries would have their taxes cut and their new equipment and machinery given a speedy tax write-off. Should this result in the introduction of automated techniques and less jobs, there were always the joys of the Leisure Society which, like Prosperity, was just around the corner.

Ah, the Leisure Society . . . For those Trudeauites skinny-dipping in Hudson Institute think-tanks, Herman Kahn provided pearls of wisdom poor Genghis could never match. C-A-N-A-D-A could spell Xanadu, if only the Perils of the Pauline Christian Work Ethic could be overcome. Restless Canadian middle-class youth, bored with the rec-room, split-level, bourgeois conformity of suburban life, wouldn't need to emulate the drug culture and the political zaniness of their class equivalents south of the border. Instead of the Yippies and "Revolution for the Hell of It," in Canada there would be the OFY-LI Pees, or evolution for the hell of it. In place of the mindless anarchy of Abby Hoffman there would be the clean-cut professionalism of the youthful Canadian Troughman—that nice kid down the block who knew the right things to do to get the people's dough to do his own thing. In Canada, the kids would not riot in the streets for all roads led to Ottawa and there the streets were paved with gold.

And if all this were not enough to build the Just Society from sea to sea, there was the ultimate panacea of the Goddess of Technique. For if society were not perfectible, man certainly was. Genetic engineering—a touch of Einstein here, a dab of Molière there, a whisper of W.C. Fields, a hint of Jim Thorpe—would create the perfect polyethnic, multicultural man and the perfect classless society of healthy minds in healthy bodies.

But if the East Block and the PMO were the Lyceum, there was little doubt of the Socratic engineer in charge. Inherited wealth, rigorous intellectual training at the world's finest schools, the broadening experience of travel, the disciplined exploration of one's inner self, the immersion into the turmoil and strife of Quebec politics, the flat refusal to accept the dictates of the past, all had combined to make Pierre Elliott Trudeau Canada's first nominee for the Socratic Academy Award. His four-year performance in the Athens of Ottawa had guaranteed him an Oscar.

By the fall of 1971 Professor Ramsay Cook officially announced that the Dominion of the North possessed only two original thinkers: one, Pierre Elliott Trudeau; the other, George M. Grant. Mr. Grant, said Mr. Cook, was, for all his Tory pessimism, a High Anglican historical materialist, a man who believed that technology and the cult of technique so overwhelmed philosophies and culture that the 1984 of the universal and homogeneous state was inevitably upon us. Mr. Trudeau, said Mr. Cook, remained the Hegelian and believed the will and mind of man could bestride technology and engineer it to useful and worthwhile ends. In this Dance of the Dialectic, Mr. Trudeau was a Waltzing Toreador; Mr. Grant a clinging wallflower.

"Until philosophers are kings, or the kings and princes of this world have the spirit and power of philosophers," Socrates had once said . . . and it had happened right here in Canada before our very eyes!

Even the Siamese Beast of nationalism-revolution had been tackled head on and tamed. In the crisis of October 1970, while others around them were losing their wits, Trudeau and the East Block Lyceumites were keeping theirs about them. The right books were read: Hannah Arendt *On Revolution,* Hans Kohn on *Nationalism,* Crane Brinton on *The Anatomy of Revolution,* William Shirer on *The Fall of the Third Republic.* The right crisis-management centres were created and the wrong-headed "bleeding hearts" and "weak-kneed" ignored. Quebec nationalist-terrorists were flushed out, a Quebec provisional-government coup nipped in the bud, a paralysis of Quebec public will cured and the seeming inevitability of separatism reduced to just one more skeleton in the Canadian closet.

The October Crisis was the Trudeau Lyceum's Finest Hour. Athens could be Sparta, for the think-tank philosophers had proved they had the courage to be kings.

Nationalism, revolution, federalism were now no longer mere philosophical abstractions but rather program concepts pragmatically tested under the ideal crisis-management conditions. The Humpty Dumpty Canadian federal state had had a slight fall, but all the Trudeau horsemen had put it together again. Henceforth, Canada would be one nation-state, not "two nations warring within the bosom of a single state." The Trudeau Philosopher-Kingdom would be peaceable, not piecemeal. One and indivisible, bilingual and multicultural.

By the summer of '72, P.E. Trudeau could rightfully claim that in Canadian politics he had made Mission Impossible the art of the possible. In the summer of 1972 "The Land Was Strong," for Trudeau had seen the future and had made it work.

Chapter Two
The Global Village Idiots

But what about the members of the Fourth Estate, the camp followers of political warfare, the gossipy fish-wives of the political marketplace? For a decade now the denizens of the Parliamentary Press Gallery had wallowed in a sea of scandal, growing fat off the avails of Rivard-Munsinger-Spencer. For them Parliament lived as they gave daily blow-by-blow accounts of the Gunfight at the Pearson-Diefenbaker Corral. Journalistic careers were made by finding bail-jumping labour leaders or bed-hopping courtesans or by proving that the Mounties were terrorizing a cancer-ridden old Commie.

Tenth-decade political culture boasted the taggle-giggle a second of "This Hour Has Seven Days," thrillers like *The Shape of Scandal* and wild westerns like *Renegade in Power* and *The Distemper of Our Times*. Unlike the Age of Trudeau, tenth-decade politics were more Neapolitan than Athenian. Instead of colloquy, comic opera.

There was no room for think-tanks in an Ottawa half-drowning in scandal. Politics was clearly the art of the possible, mere survival of the law of the day. What passed for intellectual thought in those days was the "end of ideology" thesis imported from the US and given the final stamp of absurd authority by Canada's own Marshall McLuhan. No Dance of the Dialectic here as the clash of ideas, classes, cultures dissolved into the one giant consensus of the Global Village. TV had made ideology

11

non-existent; things replaced ideas; the medium replaced the messAGE and the true intellectual was merely a weatherman, predicting and assessing "hot" and "cool."

In such a political and intellectual climate, Canada's Fourth Estate flourished. In the Carnival of tenth-decade politics, the electronic print-ants of the Parliamentary Press Gallery became the Ottawa division of the Global Village Idiots. Any highschool dropout and ex-disc jockey who could press a pencil or a pencil mike at some be-fuddled Ottawa politician caught in another inexplicable vagary was eligible for membership in Canada's journalis-tic élite corps. Neapolitan politics bred its inevitable coun-terpart—paparazzi journalism.*

Once Dief was toppled and Pearson resigned, the Boys in the Band began to worry that the Royal Musical Ride on the Rideau would soon stop as a Stanfield-Sharp decade loomed ominously on the horizon. But Trudeaumania saved the day. Pencils and pencil mikes could now record the orgiastic squeals of nubile teeny-boppers and the frenzied flutters of suburban matrons. Ottawa now seemed to be Canada's Great White Way as the Simple Neil Simons of the gallery authored their own morality play of PET the Owl and his Rittenhause-Streisand Pussycats.

But, alack, alas, the paparazzi soon discovered that the age of Trudeau was not showbusiness as usual but "mind your own business" or else. The Rittenhause fiasco not only terminated the paparazzi's maniacal love affair with Charisma Trudeau; it seemed to herald the beginning of the end of jock-strap journalism.

The shape of scandal and the ship of fools was quickly replaced by the fool- and leak-proof Trudeau dreadnaught. The paparazzi, who had previously feasted on the gourmet offerings of furniture and fraulein scandals, had to be con-tent with crumbs like the "leak" of a "secret" housing study or watch in horror as Academic Abe Rotstein pulled the biggest coup of all . . . a breath-taking advance copy

*See glossary.

of a "secret" foreign-ownership study that once again proved what every Canadian already knew.

Now the hapless paparazzi had to wrestle with strange phenomena like capital gains, depreciation and depletion allowances, standing orders, closure and the Phillips curve. Hardly the proper bread nourishment for even a third-rate flea circus, let alone the Great Forum on the Rideau.

As Athenian politics on the Hill settled in for the duration, the paparazzi found themselves in the vast nether regions of the Cave of Darkness, highschool dropouts forced to cover a continuous closed college seminar they neither understood nor liked. The dazzling sunlight of the October Crisis provided the paparazzi with a brief reprieve. But this too was a mixed blessing. Sticking pencils and mikes in front of cabinet ministers standing beside machine-gun-toting soldiers had its charms. Equally thrilling was standing in line *behind* international luminaries like CBS's Mike Wallace, the BBC's Robert McNeill, the *New Yorker*'s Edith Iglauer and commando units from *Newsweek, Time* and *Der Speigel* for Charisma Trudeau interviews, declamations and aphorisms.

But there was also the horror of having to wrestle with portentous phrases like "apprehended popular insurrection," "Peace, Order and Good Government," "coup d'état" and "provisional government." Those paparazzi who thought Lord Acton was the first mayor of a small Ontario town understandably had great difficulty recognizing that Trudeau meant Claude Ryan when he stood the Actonian dictum on its head, announcing that lack of power tends to corrupt and absolute lack of power tends to corrupt absolutely.

Perhaps they thought the aphorisms applied to them. In Pearsonian days the paparazzi had power, as they dealt with the frail, fallible but likeable Pre-Raphaelite LBP. Now the paparazzi faced the Jacobin, the unlikeable but Incorruptible Robespierre Trudeau, who was making sure the separatist bastard child of the Quiet Revolution was a stillbirth, without even the courtesy of calling on them to act as clucking and approving midwives.

But even the dazzling sunlight of the October Crisis had to set. Once again the paparazzi were loose fish in a sea of "designated areas," tax credits and the growth in the participation rate of the labour force. In this Periclean atmosphere it was inevitable that tenth-decade paparazzi would give way to the sweet smell of the Newthink piece on the op-ed page.

Chapter Three
Punditi-in, Punditi-out and Radical Chicci

Pundits per se, of course, were not new to the Ottawa political scene. Laurier had his Willison and Dafoe; King his Dexter and Hutchison; St. Laurent, his Fraser; Diefenbaker, his Nicholson; Pearson his Newman. But these prowlers in the corridors of power were primarily interested in politics, in the clash of political ideals and in the men who embraced or denied them. They were either hagiographers or muckrakers, sometimes surrogate politicians, but always compulsive members in the cult of the political personality.

But the punditi* who found favour in the new Trudeau era were men of sterner stuff. They were certainly not the authors of the Oakes-Harbron-Peacock brand of instant Trudeau puff books which no self-respecting Trudeaucrat, least of all Trudeau himself, would ever admit to reading. Also relegated to the punditi-out basket in the PMO were melodramatists like Peter Newman, scurrilous "naughties" like Doug Fisher and George Bain and Southam columnist Charles Lynch, whom one Trudeaucrat described wistfully as "the poor man's Scotty Reston."

The punditi-in basket of the PMO contained a hodge-podge of academic journalists and journalistic-academics. The Toronto *Star*'s Tony Westell could ponder the paradox that was Trudeau from the vantage point of a comfortable Regency chair in an East Block office. Ram-

*See glossary.

say Cook could pledge allegiance to *The Maple Leaf Forever* in the very presence of Trudeau himself. The Montreal *Star*'s Bill Wilson, *Time* Magazine's Geoffrey Stevens, the Toronto *Star*'s Peter Desbarats, the *Financial Post*'s Clive Baxter and the others allowed access to the think-tanks in the East Block Lyceum inevitably became Lyceumites themselves. Soon they could be seen in the parliamentary restaurant, looking down their noses at their more uncouth press colleagues as they lunched with a fellow Lyceumite and debated the intricacies of some new technique of economic forecasting or some new principle of public administration.

It would be unfair to characterize this delicate arrangement as news management, conscious or otherwise. Rather it was a meeting of minds on the one hand and an exclusion of non-minds on the other.

The punditi-in shared, with the prime minister, a respect for good taste and breeding and a desire to see both politics and journalism cleansed of their impurities to become, in essence, proper callings in the finest Christian sense of that term. Trudeau's own initial view of journalism was certainly coloured by the edifying contrast his own *Cité Libre* provided to the payola-kept press of the Duplessis régime. His view of the Parliamentary Press Gallery was less harsh but at the same time less flattering. The Quebec paparazzi at least had the intelligence of the corrupt. To Trudeau, the Ottawa paparazzi were simply mindless and ignorant.

It certainly bothered him that these electronic print-ants were purported to have had the collective power to lift him from Lilliputian obscurity to the Gulliverian heights. Certainly no interviewer's question could more quickly earn the full Trudeau gripe of wrath than the one that even hinted that he had been propelled into power by the thrust of the paparazzi.

As a good Hegelian, he was aware of the paparazzi

as an evil necessity; as a tough and rigorous intellectual he was aware that, for the most part, they were functional illiterates. If the Ottawa paparazzi wouldn't read his *Federalism and the French-Canadians* (as, for the most part, they didn't) why should he read or listen to their stuff?

But what particularly irked Trudeau about the Ottawa Press Gallery (Anglophone division) was their all-pervasive ignorance of Francophonia, its people, culture and language. He was aware that, to the paparazzi, Quebec was either a winter carnival or an FLQ circus. If they didn't quite view French Canadians as the White Niggers of North America, they, at their Lily St. Cyr-est best, viewed French Canadians to be as newsworthy (and in the same way) as the black niggers of Watts and Newark.

As for the Francophone division of the gallery, to Trudeau they were at worst separatists, at best provincial parochialists clinging to their Quebec ghetto walls for whatever nourishment and comfort this garrison mentality could provide.

Trudeau expected better from the illuminati wing (Anglophone) of the gallery. But there too he found a web of fuzzy thinking. The illuminati (particularly most of the punditi-out and the radical chicci and some punditi-in) were either ignorant of the zenophobia inherent in all nationalism and particularly French Canada's, or worse, were willing to tolerate or encourage French-Canadian nationalism through concepts like "Associate State" and "Two Nations." Certain radical chicci even had the chutzpah to suggest that he was more Elliott than Trudeau, a pseudo-French Canadian who did not understand his own people and even worse was the one true barrier to their proper aspirations.

These initial irritations, however, were only temporary. Trudeaumania and the proportions of the 1968 One Canada triumph had already proved that most Anglophones bought the Trudeau view of Quebec's proper place in Confederation. Trudeau's handling of the October Crisis had brought that support in Anglophonia to near-universal proportions. In Francophonia, Trudeau's obvious native-son status (obvious to every Francophone except the separatists and their Anglophone radical-chicci allies) and his display of courage at the St. Jean Baptiste Day riot had, in 1968, already won him that "chez nous" infatuation Francophones always reserve for strong leaders. His masterful handling of the FLQ crisis had heightened that infatuation into a veritable Love Story, Francophone-style.

Trudeau, the intellectual, had always lamented that nativist sentimental streak in his racial confrères; Trudeau, the charismatic leader, was unabashedly prepared to live with it. The response of Francophones to his handling of the October Crisis was all the more palatable to Trudeau because it convincingly proved to both the illuminati and the paparazzi in the Parliamentary Press Gallery that he, Trudeau, could win overwhelming public support in both Francophonia and Anglophonia without the media's vaunted influence and aid. During and immediately after the October Crisis most Anglophone punditi-out and radical chicci on the Hill were willing to say "mea culpa" for their past heresies and sins on la bella phenomena Francophonia. Associate State and Two Nations talk disappeared on the Hill. Nor was such talk revived when, months after the crisis, the punditi-out and radical chicci had sufficiently recovered their composure to declaim as conventional wisdom that the Trudeau handling of the October Crisis was at worst an anti-separatist plot, at best a horrendous tampering with our traditional liberties and rights.

With Quebec once again firmly riveted to the bedrock of Confederation, Trudeau could return to the joys of the Just Society and the cult of excellence. Trudeau and his fellow Hegelians in the East Block were sufficiently materialist in their outlook to realize that our economy and our culture were too locked in to the multinational dynamics of the universal and homogeneous state to provide a proper outlet for what was truly unique in the Canadian psyche. What they were quick to perceive was that the one thing that was truly ours was the Canadian state apparatus itself. In a world of bureaucratic jungles governed only by the rules of Parkinson's law, Canadians could with glowing hearts and true patriot love build the world's finest civil service, bilingual and all. The cosmic universe of bureaucracy could be put in proper orbit around Ottawa's sun-king philosopher as he and the Lyceumites came up with the immutable principles and heavenly images of proper public administration. (It was in the Trudeau years that an award was offered for the country's *best* civil servant and the Order of Canada was always peppered with a steady dose of honoured civil servants.)

Surely such an enterprise was worth doing and worth doing well. The punditi-in quickly appreciated the magnitude of the task, joined in and were welcomed. For one thing they understood the essential link between Canada's world leadership in the arts of public administration and Trudeau's theory of participatory politics. In an age of super-technology, good politics was no more than the art of problem-solving by good government management. To participate fully in the new political process the public had to understand the problems and realize they were being solved. This they could best do vicariously—through trust in the punditi-in whose easy access to the East Block Lyceum had made them aware of the magnitude of the problems faced and the obvious finesse with which they had been tackled.

In this natural order of things there was, by definition, no room for the paparazzi, whose view of participatory democracy was to provide the public with vicarious thrills like which lady was the PM shedding, which one was he wedding. No room, either, for the punditi-out, who did not seem to know what was really going on or, if they did, seemed for reasons unfathomable to feel the effort not worth reporting.

Some punditi-out, scandal of scandals, even had the chutzpah to suggest that what was going on was worth doing but was *not* being done well. For example, Professor James Eayrs, whose intellectual credentials for philosopher-kingship were at least the equal of the prime minister's and whose "common touch" with the toiling masses at least rivalled that of Ivan Head, pronounced Mr. Trudeau to be a "dilettante in power." This exercise in punditry set all Ottawa agog and for weeks Lyceumites, Rockcliffites and ex-Oxford dons debated the question: Does a dilettante lacking power *tend* to be less corrupt than a dilettante with power or does a dilettante lacking power *tend* to be an absolute bore?

Doug Fisher, the socialist ex-MP, never tired of recording the petite flaws and mini-bloopers of the Lyceumites. Walter Stewart, eldest scion of a fine old Ontario socialist family and a man whose inherited faith in the marvels of mandarin economic management knew no bounds, had the turgid temerity to suggest there were not enough Baptists in the East Block think-fount. "Supergroup," he suggested, was hogging the pool and not letting the regular deputy ministers and old career bureaucrats join in on the walking of the waters.

Even worse, Eric Kierans charged that certain cabinet ministers were being barred from the baptismal font. He resigned his cabinet post to become a tireless, if sometimes indecipherable, punditi-out himself.

Still, all in all, these were minor aberrations. Once the Quebec crisis was over, and the PM's March 5th, 1971 wedding put an end to what vestigial remains of

Trudeaumania still existed, the charisma phase of Trudeau politics was over. The Trudeau Greeks were now bearing gifts of Periclean wisdom, dazzling excellences, permanent in nature.

On Parliament Hill time stood still as the Peace Tower ticked off one administrative triumph after another. And slowly but surely it began to dawn on the paparazzi-electronic-print-ants on the Hill that the Trudeau administration was strictly bread and no circus, and—wonder of wonders—dull, dull, dull! The horrors of a Stanfield-Sharp decade anticipated had now been realized in the new after-charisma clean-shave Trudeau age.

Post Charisma:
Trudeau and the
New National Mood

Chapter Four
From the Good Old Seven Days to the Brightest and the Best

The new Trudeau dullness took some time for the punditi, radical chicci and paparazzi of the gallery to get used to. After all, most of them hadn't had to survive in the sleepwalking politics of St. Laurent, nor fend for themselves in the Hampstead maze verbiage of Mackenzie King. Both these right honourable gentlemen were pre-electronic and pre-McLuhan. In those Hesiodic days, if a medium had a message it was strictly for the eyes and ears of the prime minister himself.

The eyes and ears of the nation only got into the act with the Canadian television explosion that began in the early fifties and reached its zenith by the late sixties. Fortunately, Canada's fascination with television seemed to reach its apex at the very time that Diefenbaker could provide the home screens of the nation with an authentic Canadian Paranoid Pa Cartwright, and Pearson with follies that would make Mr. Ziegfeld turn green with envy.

American TV shows were providing dramatic conflict, comedy and sex. For Canadian TV to compete in this kind of marketplace it needed something equally dramatic, equally funny and equally sexy. The confrontation politics of Diefenbaker and Pearson bred the inevitable confrontation television of "This Hour Has Seven Days." The accusatory shotgun mike poking at the squirming Ottawa politician had all the needed phallic overtones of good hard political porno. (If phallic symbolism wouldn't

suffice, there was always the actual "soft" porno of Mun-
singer and Sevigny to keep TV viewers alert.) Seven Days
deliberately promoted itself as public affairs that was both
entertainment and fun and by 1964 Canadians were certainly ready for a good hearty laugh and the occasional
jolt of a voyeur's voltage. The Canadian public had been
made comatose by the linch-pinhead greyness of Mackenzie
King and the nice nellyism of middle-powermanship.
Canadians were grateful for the honest, competent and
business-minded government of C.D. Howe-Winters-St.
Laurent, but big-business government wasn't exactly
showbusiness government; not, at least, until the pipeline
scandal. Even then, had the techniques of television been
as developed as they were a decade later, one can hardly
envisage a shotgun mike pointing up the nose of nice
Uncle Louis, president of the Company That Was Canada,
or up the snout of snarly old C.D. Howe, its rough-tough
chairman of the board.

It may have been historical irony or historical necessity,
but it seemed that the full flowering of Canadian confrontation television came at the same time as the decomposi-
tion of Canadian politics in the Diefenbaker-Pearson era.
Perhaps one was fertilizer for the other.

The mistake Canadian broadcasters and the media
generally made was to believe that confrontation politics
would remain a permanent feature of the Canadian political scene. It may have been another historical irony or
one more conjurer's trick of the Goddess of Necessity
that Pierre Elliott Trudeau was chosen leader of the Liberal
party the very week that Martin Luther King was assas-
sinated. By 1968 Canadians were saturated with the
Watts-Newark-Detroit violence from south of the border
spilling over on to their TV screens. They were also getting
a bit jaded with the antics of the aging gunfighters at
the Pearson-Diefenbaker Corral—gunfighters who were
neither dying nor slowly fading away.

By the spring of 1968 the majority of Canadians were urban or suburban, more mobile and sophisticated than ever before. They were no longer living-room, rec-room habitués, with eyes perpetually glued to their TV sets. They no longer regarded the box as "magic," particularly in the areas of news and public affairs. They realized that the world was too dangerous a place ever again to find public affairs, even of the domestic kind, really "entertaining." Urban Canadians of the emerging seventies no longer wanted a prime minister (or an opposition leader, for that matter) who would harangue them; nor did they want a prime minister whose affability under duress made him appear vulnerable and somehow made *them* feel guilty.

By the spring of 1968 Canadians wanted a prime minister they could like and respect, one who looked invulnerable and who could make *them* feel invulnerable. Trudeau fitted the public mood perfectly. Trudeaumania was far more the media's instinctive response to the new public mood than a media-induced state of public frenzy.

Canadians now wanted an end to confrontation politics and confrontation journalism. They wanted more of that good old Centennial-Expo feeling. They were ready for Oneness—One Canada, Justice, the Just Society and Love... Love... Love. Only the paparazzi instinctively understood this new public mood. Thus it was no accident that during the Czech crisis of 1968, when the world stood on the brink of total nuclear war, the first question a paparazznik asked Trudeau, who had just rushed back to Ottawa from a summer holiday, was whether or not he had been secretly married.

The last to catch on to the new public mood were the punditi-out and the radical chicci, particularly those in the broadcasting field. They still believed that confrontation journalism was important, and something the public still clamoured for, like in the good old Seven Days.

But the question they failed to ask and answer for themselves was: confront *whom* and for *what?* The Trudeau government was singularly free from corruption, incompetence and timidity. There were no more fraulein and furniture scandals. Nor was there the what's-good-for-big-business-is-good-for-the-country atmosphere of the St. Laurent years. Neither were there the Uncle Tomish implications of the King-St. Laurent years that French-Canadians were temperamentally unsuited for certain portfolios. Instead of a C.D. Howe or a Bob Winters, a Pépin, a Marchand, a Cadieux held major economic and defence portfolios.

Gone too was a fear of government intervention or an undue respect for the old WASP Rockcliffe élites that dominated Ottawa's civil service. Trudeau's was an *activist* government, flatly refusing to admit that *any* problem was insoluble or that the problem-solvers had to be of the King-St. Laurent vintage. Under its banner, a host of talented Francophones, multiculturalphones and just plain bright new people were being recruited into the civil service.

Above all, the Trudeau government was a self-confident, assertive administration. Its ministers didn't squint or look guilty on television, nor were there the self-deprecations and diplomatic niceties of the previous administration. Instead of peace-making, the Trudeau government preferred the martial arts. War—against inflation, against separatism, against nationalism, against Pearson-prissy-sissy internationalism.

How does one confront a government combining Periclean wisdom and Spartan courage? Impossible! Television shows that tried the old confrontation technique on Trudeau cabinet ministers found their ratings plunging, their audiences succumbing to deep slumber. Those broadcasters-punditi-out-radical chicci who tried taking on Trudeau himself found themselves slashed to ribbons.

And, horror of horrors, they found their audience alert and awake and cheering Trudeau on.

It was a brand new ballgame, politicians making the journalists look silly and the public loving it. What equally floored the punditi-out and the radical chicci was that they branded the Trudeauites as "arrogant" and the public didn't seem to care.

This public response flew in the face of Canadian history. Sir John A. was drunken and wise; Alexander Mackenzie sober and dull; Sir Wilfrid sober and Silver-Foxy sly; Borden, dour and determined; Meighen, unrevised, unrepentant—and forever snowed under by Mackenzie King, forever revised, repentant and *there*.

What the punditi-out and radical chicci did not seem to realize was that the Canadian people themselves were undergoing changes. The age of Mackenzie King was not only dead in Ottawa but all over the country. Canadians were no longer Uriah Heepish but rather Great Forward Leapish. Our North American affluence, minus the Vietnam-race-riots-assassination-pollution syndrome of our neighbours to the south, had given birth to a new Canadian phenomenon: self-love. The Canadian Identity, hitherto lost in the lacunae of British Connection colonialism and Roosevelt Good Neighbour continentalism, had at long last been found in the New Canadian Nationalism.

By 1964 Canadians were already cocky and arrogant and getting more so every day. Pearson's inability to grab the nettle of this new mood irritated Canadians. "This Hour Has Seven Days" sensed the new mood and made the most of it. Cocky Canadians loved Cocky Pat and Cocky Laurier as they made mincemeat of Pearson chickens coming home to roost.

Trudeau was something else again. In the early Trudeau years, the lady from Wadena, Saskatchewan, could go to the town drugstore and see Trudeau peering down at her from the cover of *Newsweek* or *Time*. Flipping the pages she could see American cartoonists depicting a sleek, sybaritic Trudeau driving his Mercedes by a stalled *Grapes of Wrath* vintage dump truck carrying North America's two biggest bores, Hube the Hump and Tricky Dicky.

At last *our* leader was interesting and alive; *their* leaders moribund and dull. At last *we* were interesting and alive; the Yankees moribund and dull. Canadian confrontation journalism in such an atmosphere was not only unworkable but really an affront to our new-found national sensibilities.

The Canadian punditi-out and radical chicci may have been out of touch with this new national sensibility, but our political leaders were not. Robert Stanfield, fully realizing that his style and approach were bad television, was equally aware that television was not the *entire* political ballgame. He sensed the public's lack of enthusiasm for confrontation politics. He also knew that while the sheriff who replaced Wyatt Earp in Tombstone was not as memorable as his predecessor, he certainly lasted a lot longer. A continuation of Diefenbaker gunfighter tactics, Stanfield realized, could only spell Tombstone for the Conservative party.

Stanfield let the more colourful Diefenbaker flail away impotently at the ever-waiting TV cameras while he went quietly about the business of rebuilding his party as (to quote the cynics) the incredible alternative to the incomparable Trudeau. Stamina and patience were Stanfield's trump cards. He was prepared to endure the loneliness of the long-distance runner while he patiently waited for Trudeau, the sprinter, to trip over that one hurdle too many.

Trudeau too sensed the new public mood and was prepared to use it as the shock absorber for the many, many things he wanted done and done *right away*. Trudeau was intelligent, honest, very moral and very Hegelian. He was certainly not the crafty, Machiavellian, power-hungry, professional politico his more mindless media and political critics insisted he was. There was little, if any, of the Wily Coyote in him, but one hell of a lot of the irrepressible Road Runner.

This prime minister was a philosopher-king, not a Mackenzie King. There were no touches of "War Measures if necessary, but not necessarily War Measures" in the Trudeau approach. Nor did this supposed Machiavellian call an election at the height of his post-October Crisis popularity as a Sir John A., a King, a Duplessis or a Diefenbaker would, in similar circumstances, most assuredly have done.

Trudeau was neither a demagogue nor a professional politician. He was a gifted intellectual but a political amateur, more interested in the arts of governing than in the perpetual political arts of out-manoeuvring opponents and winning elections. He was certainly more St. Laurent and Alexander Mackenzie than Laurier and Mackenzie King.

Trudeau also sensed that the new public mood of cockiness and arrogance was very similar to his own mood, which many branded as arrogant but which was really a combination of a sense of self-worth and, conversely, a sense of shyness and a desire to be left alone. Trudeau chose to interpret the new public mood to be a mandate for patriotism rather than anti-American nationalism, for a strong central government rather than a putting of Quebec in its place, and for a strong reform legislative thrust in areas too long neglected—tax reform, regional disparities, monopoly domination of the marketplace. In foreign affairs he interpreted the new mood to call for a policy that reflected both Canadian pride and Canadian shyness, i.e., an active role in Cold War détente through closer ties with Russia and China, and a correspondingly lesser involvement in NATO and UN, brokerage politics plus a vigorous assertion of sovereignty in the Arctic and other coastal waters in the areas of pollution, fishing and oil exploration.

This Trudeau reading of the new public mood may have been wrong in one or indeed all of these specifics. But one aspect of the new public mood was patently clear to Trudeau and to all the other politicians on the Hill: the country wanted to be governed and clearly felt Trudeau to be the best man for the job.

One more thing was equally clear—the Canadian public would brook no interference from the media in what at long last seemed to be Canada's century. What Laurier had promised Canadians in the 1900s Trudeau would surely deliver in the seventies if only the electronic-print-ants would return to the dunghill and leave Parliament Hill to the Brightest and the Best.

Trudeau's contempt for the press simply mirrored the public's contempt. In the new Athenian scheme of things, which the public was clearly buying, the members of the Fourth Estate were a mathematical marvel. Within fifty yards of the Commons Chamber, in the very heart of Parliament Hill, they were to be even *less* than nobodies.

Chapter Five
Bread on the Waters
of the Rideau

But even ants have to eat to live. Was there to be no bread at all on the waters of the Rideau? Yes and no. In the good old Seven Days of confrontation politics and confrontation journalism the making of bread by paparazzi, punditi and radical chicci was a simple affair. Trudeaumania was a natural breadwinner for the paparazzi and certainly for those punditi and radical chicci who, playing God and liking it, chose to cast Trudeau in their own image. The October Crisis was pure chips and gravy for one and all, particularly for the paparazzi and the radical chicci and punditi who, once again playing God, could now cast Lucifer Trudeau from the Pundits' Paradise they had all once lovingly shared.

But the post-October, post-bachelorhood and post-charisma Trudeau emerging in the spring of 1971 seemed to portend seven lean and hungry years of empty media fleshpots. Fortified by its own resolve and that of the public's to end confrontation politics, post-charisma Trudeau big-seminar government became as efficient, as politically untouchable and every bit as uninspiring as St. Laurent's big-business government. Both Trudeau, the no-nonsense intellectual, and C.D. Howe-St. Laurent, the no-nonsense "business-as-usual" men, had each in their own way mastered the problems of running a country with a mixed economy and a mixed racial heritage. Each had in their own way provided good government.

But as one of Trudeau's most trusted aides succinctly put it to one of the more jaded members of the Press Gallery one fine Ottawa summer afternoon: "Good government is dull government." What perhaps that aide and other Trudeaucrats did not realize was that post-charisma Trudeau, good and dull, was, like good and dull Uncle Louis before him, bringing the game of politics to a standstill. The C.D. Howe-Bob Winters ivory hunters of Brazilian Traction had been replaced by the donnish ivory-tower management of Oxford Robertson and Harvard Head but in both cases politics had become 99 and 44/100 per cent as pure and 99 and 44/100 per cent as bland as Ivory soap.

In this kind of process Trudeau was running the risk of becoming a bore, as big a bore as good and dull Uncle Louis had become in 1957. The trouble with bores in the perpetual game that is politics is that bores, by definition, are not "newsworthy."

"Newsworthiness" is, of course, the stuff that journalists traditionally live on. In the mid thirties, at the height of the turbulent Depression, there was enough of the stuff going around to sustain thirty-seven Ottawa journalists, the full membership of the gallery in 1935-36. In the mid forties, with Ottawa seething in conscription crises and military fiascoes, there was enough of it to sustain a gallery membership of forty-five. By 1971, tenth-decade politics plus Trudeaumania and the October Crisis had provided enough "stuff" to sustain the livelihood of 125 members of the Parliamentary Press Gallery.

By the summer of 1971 there wasn't enough "stuff" to sustain the livelihood of a Tom Thumb or a Tiny Tim, let alone 125 full-grown adults, many with wives, kids and lovers to feed. The spectre of unemployment began to stalk the corridor halls leading from the gallery to the Commons chamber. There was even dire talk that the gallery's "secret" bar might have to be converted into a soup kitchen.

But all the scare talk was for nought. What the gallery had failed to perceive was the silver lining in the cloud of the new Canadian mood. The new Canadian nationalism had repudiated confrontation politics and confrontation journalism but it had embraced all things Canadian. Under the umbrella of Canadian content, not only writers, playwrights and poets, but punditi, radical chicci and paparazzi could find shelter.

CRTC Canadian-content rulings alone had made the electronic ants viable. Radio and TV stations, desperately trying to fill their Canadian quotient, were willing to take whatever the paparazzi and punditi were saying, no matter how thoughtful, dull, mindless or numbing, as long as it was said by a Canadian about Canada. Canadian content became the great loss leader in the marketplace of Canadian TV and radio.

In these new arrangements, everyone was reasonably happy. The punditi-in could fill the op-ed pages with their Newthink pieces on the wonders of Lyceum legislation. The paparazzi could churn out the post-charisma Trudeau ministerial statements, thirty seconds or less, with their own opening and closing on-air statements providing whatever balm their frail egos needed. The radical chicci, invariably members in good standing of the Canadian Establishment, could, on the People's Network, gently chide the Lyceumites for their lack of radical fervour and still remain in the good books of one and all.

As for the punditi-out, they too could survive. With Stanfield refusing to come out of his corner and fight and Tommy Douglas about to hang up his bantam-weight championship gloves, the punditi-out could persuade their proprietors that they were fulfilling a time-honoured journalistic tradition, that of Her Majesty's Disloyal Unofficial Opposition.

Still, if post-charisma Trudeauland was no famine, it

was certainly no feast. Gallery members, like all good
Canadians, had both their collective and individual sense
of pride. As good Canadians, they realized that Trudeau
was providing the best of all possible government; but
as self-respecting journalists they didn't like their new
role of "imaginative" re-writing of government press re-
leases on such non-newsworthy items as "Innovation and
the Structure of Canadian Industry" or "The New Industrial Strategy."

What the gallery yearned for, especially the paparazzi,
was the newsworthy glitter of Gerda Gold or, at the very
least, the old Trudeau tinsel of Charisma Camelot Days
of Yore. The Ottawa paparazzi were particularly bitter
about Trudeau sneaking off to Vancouver to wed his
young Guinevere, letting the Pacific rat pack get all the
glory that was by turf-right theirs. Their wrath was well
nigh uncontainable when they discovered that the prime
minister's connubial bliss was not to be sacramentally
shared with them.

What little communion there still existed between them
was disappearing rapidly in the face of this kind of betrayal. Nor did relations improve any when, on the rare
occasions post-charisma Trudeau himself agreed to face
the paparazzi, he would either tie their questions up in
knots or rebuke them for the ignorance upon which they
were based.

Chapter Six
Two Canadas—
Diefenbaker's and Trudeau's

In the good old charisma days this Trudeau put-down of paparazzi ignorance provided the peasant paps with the kind of sado-masochistic pleasures the hapless opposition parties enjoyed in the prosperous dull St. Laurent days, when C.D. Howe would rebuke them for their ignorance of "sound business practices." In the post-charisma period, neither Trudeau nor the paparazzi were happy with the old sado-masochist relationship.

What the paparazzi never knew (and still don't) was that Trudeau never *really* enjoyed the charisma phase of his political career. The irrational aspects of it all went against the very grain of his rational, scholarly, one could almost say scholastic nature. The irrational aspects of Trudeaumania were too close to the kind of thoughtless quest-for-authority politics he had fought against in Duplessis's Quebec for so many years.

Nor did Trudeaumania provide the right kind of thought-out and careful ripostes to the careful and thought-out arguments of the separatists. What Trudeau wanted from Canadians was a commitment to his views based on conviction, not passion—a commitment derived from a careful reading of his *Federalism and the French Canadians* rather than an emotional Beatleswoon response to his mere physical presence.

Equally repulsive to Trudeau were some of the more calculating aspects that underlay Trudeaumania. He was aware that many Anglophones shared the view of Judge J.T. Thorson, the western Viking Liberal, who supported

Trudeau at the 1968 convention because Trudeau would, to quote the judge, "put Quebec in its proper place." Trudeau realized too that many Canadians, particularly in western Canada, were interpreting his One Canada to be on a par with the call for un-hyphenated Canadianism that John Diefenbaker had been preaching as gospel throughout his entire political career.

There was always one hell of a difference between Dief's One Canada and Trudeau's, a difference Trudeau, Pelletier and Marchand were always aware of and a difference that only gradually dawned on Diefenbaker and his followers in western Canada. The One Canada Diefenbaker envisaged was a baptismal melting pot into which the Cherniaks, the Caccias, the Paproskis, the Cardinals, the Chrétiens, the Guays, the Diefenbakers and the Campbell-Bannermans were to be immersed, miraculously coming out un-hyphenated Canadians. The trouble was that the distilled Canadian that came out of this kind of One Canada melting pot was to be at least fifty-one per cent Campbell-Bannerman or, to put it in more spirited terms, more Seagram than Bronfman.

The un-hyphenated Canadian was to be a WASP manqué on the streets and an ethnic at home. In this vertical mosiac, WASP culture was to reign supreme. The Queen was to be the Great White Mother uniting us all, those of Cree breed and the Hebrew creed, the Slav and the Teuton, the WASP Beauty and the Beastly Frog (who is secretly a Prince and once you tell him you really love him, becomes one and takes his rightful place to the left and just below the throne of the Great White Queen).

In this One Canada, Quebec was a Louisiana if necessary, but not necessarily Louisiana. In any event, many of these kinds of One Canadians were now prepared for the sake of national unity to start telling Newfie jokes in place of the old habitant and honkie ones, proving that in the new un-hyphenated Canada, *some* Anglo-Saxons were dumber than *some* of the lesser breeds.

Trudeau's One Canada contained none of these elements. There were no lesser breeds in his scheme of things, no intention of putting Quebec in its place, and certainly no intention of ever seeing Quebec become a Louisiana (no matter what his radical-chicci critics might say).

The only thing Trudeau's One Canada shared with Diefenbaker's was the desire to put Quebec's ultranationalists and separatists in their place. This indeed was Trudeau's central purpose from the day he took the oath of office. To Trudeau, separatist philosophy would accomplish for Quebec the very thing that would most endanger its very existence: the Louisiana atrophy of a tiny, separate French state, loose in a giant English-speaking North American sea. What Trudeau was offering Francophonia was as old as the Laurier formula: total equality for Francophones all across Canada.

And this fifty-fifty equality was no longer to be given as an act of generosity on the part of Anglophonia, but as a right fully earned. Trudeau's French Canadians were no longer the simple habitants of Drummond's poetry; nor were talented French Canadians British on the streets and ethnic at home, as they had to be in Sir Wilfrid's day. Neither were they any longer the brilliant but emotional lawyers, poets and priests of yore.

Trudeau's French Canadians were as brilliant and as hard-headed as their English-Canadian counterparts. The new urban-suburban Québécois had more than his share of degrees in economics, business and public administration. The salons of the Quebec bourgeoisie were as elegant as their Parisian counterparts and the conversation in them every bit as technocratic as in the best Servan-Schreiber circles.

This new Quebec bourgeoisie certainly considered itself at the very least the equal of its English-Canadian equiva-

lent. Indeed, many members of this new Quebec bourgeoisie had the same contempt for the English-Canadian
upper and middle classes as their Parisian equivalents had
for the British Heath-ridden bourgeoisie, pleading for
entry into the European Common Market as the only sure
guarantee of its continued existence. For the new Quebec
bourgeoisie, the Louisiana role envisaged for it in the
Diefenbaker One Canada was anathema and the Great
White Mother of Monarchy a patent absurdity, if not a
complete affront.

The only options open were the technocratic-
bureaucratic delights that the Parizeau Péquistes were pro-
mising in Laurentia-Quebec or the technocratic bureaucratic delights being offered in Ottawa by a Trudeau One
Canada that was bilingual and bicultural. It was either
the segregation of separate but equal or the integration
of federalism and equal.

If the latter option were chosen, it would be a fifty-fifty
proposition, half Anglophone, half Francophone. Diefenbaker's One Canada, Campbell-Bannerman style, would
be fitted, melting pot and all, into the half-Canada that
Anglophonia could call its own. Francophonia would
remain one hundred per cent French and free from the
constant boil and bubble, toil and trouble witches' brew
that often emanates from melting pots. In this federalist
option, the new One Canada would require neutral symbols, like a Maple Leaf rather than a Red Ensign, Police
rather than the Royal Canadian Mounted Police, and
perhaps an elected president rather than a hereditary
monarch.

In this respect the Quebec One Canadians shared the
view of their separatist rivals that the old British traditions
and symbols had little if any utilitarian value to the Quebec
bourgeoisie. And both sides agreed that the battle between
the two options was a utilitarian one.

The Péquistes argued for separation first and negotiations for a new Canadian Common Market—if necessary, but not necessarily—second. The Quebec One Canadians argued that Confederation had already provided the needed Canadian Common Market and Quebeckers could be at the throttle of it as efficiently as France was at the throttle of the EEC. And both sides of this fierce argument, raging within the bosom of the Quebec bourgeoisie, knew that whatever option was chosen, the ballgame now being played was fundamentally different from the one that had been played for decades before. The Egyptian fleshpots provided by "les rois nègres" of Duplessis and St. Laurent were being replaced by the promised land of the philosopher-kings, Parizeau-Lévesque or Trudeau-Pelletier.

In the white heat of Trudeaumania and the October Crisis, these distinctions between the two One Canadas were lost sight of by most Canadians, English and French, and by most journalists, paparazzi and otherwise. First charisma and then strongman politics were called for to keep the country together, and both were delivered. But in the calm post-charisma Trudeau period, what the prime minister was trying to show the press, the business community and the country was that his One Canada was the right One Canada. The superb performance of his Quebec compatriots in the Lyceum That Was Canada was all the proof necessary that French Canadians were equal to English Canadians and could manage our country and our economy just as well. Trudeau was proving that Francophones could be as hard-headed, as pragmatic, as business-minded and as dull, dull, dull as the traditional Canadian WASP.

In particular, Trudeau was trying to show Canada's business élites that they had nothing to fear from a federal government in which artful French-Canadian practitioners of the cult of excellence held the dominant sway. True, Trudeau himself and most of his ministers (with the exception of Brazilian Traction Sharp and Bob Andras) had never run a business themselves. But wasn't Trudeau himself the son of that rarest of breeds, a self-made French-Canadian millionaire entrepreneur (not to mention the son-in-law of that not-so-rare breed, a self-made Anglo-Saxon millionaire entrepreneur)?

Wasn't it the business community and not the labour leaders who were willing to lay down their profits and join them in the War Against Inflation? Wasn't he also, as his Boswell, Ramsay Cook, pointed out, the one Canadian intellectual who had no fear of the Goddess of Technique? Technology posed no terrors for Trudeau, Pelletier and Lalonde and it never had for Canada's future- and profit-oriented business and corporate élites.

Trudeau and his Quebec disciples had always disavowed the buy-back-Canada arguments of the Watkins-Gordon school of economic nationalism. The past was to be buried but the future of technology was to be ours. If a competition bill or a cabinet minister needed to be dumped in the process, so be it. If the corporations needed tax cuts to be "competitive" and future-oriented, so be it too.

Surely one thing was clear in the new post-charisma Trudeau age: in the next election to come, Trudeau would be re-elected, as one close Trudeau aide put it, because he had provided the best management team in the country. In the next election Trudeau would be ratified by the stockholder electorate because the Trudeau One Canada worked. Its balance sheet was in the black and the country showed a profit. In the next election it was to be mind over matter. The hard-headed Puritan-ethic WASPS would buy the hard-headed Puritan-ethic Trudeau team as the only way to keep the Canadian Common Market working and making a buck for one and all. If the paparazzi didn't understand the true dimensions of these new proven theorems, surely the business-oriented, technology-loving

Anglophones would.

In the new symbiotic relationship of the two Puritan ethics, the apparent idiocy of the paparazzi was not only a superfluity but a downright nuisance. The ego of post-charisma Trudeau demanded a reasoned, pragmatic endorsement by the Canadian people of a reasonable, pragmatic government. Plaza Pierre was now married and four years older; indeed, by the spring of 1972 older than any other government leader in the country, as the Canadian Press paparazzi fondly pointed out.

Four years before, Trudeau didn't really have the stomach for charismatic politics but, like a good Hegelian, did what necessity demanded of him. Now, four years later, he didn't really have the stamina and certainly not the inclination for jet-propulsion plaza politics. What stamina and inclination didn't rule out, the dignity imposed upon him by his new role as husband and father-to-be certainly did. (What Andy Hardy could get away with was unthinkable for Pop Hardy, the judge.)

The political universe Trudeau saw unfolding before him was a calm and dignified one with rainbows everywhere and not a cloud in sight. The next election would be a stockholders' meeting, and those traditionally were closed to the press or, in the Trudeaucrat view, should be. Still, politics wasn't quite business and even Trudeau's entrenched Bill of Rights guaranteed freedom of the press to the licentious paparazzi.

But that same Bill of Rights guaranteed him the right to conduct the next election as he saw fit. Trudeau was going to conduct his dignified dialogue with the Canadian people and the paparazzi be damned. They would be confined to the vast nether regions of the PM's campaign jet. The next campaign would be won without them and the vaunted power of the electronic print-ants would prove to be the myth that he, in his heart of hearts, had always known it to be.

Storming the Gates
of the Lyceum

Chapter Seven
The Revolt of the
Peasant Paparazzi

If post-charisma Trudeau was too sure of himself and too bored to continue the old sado-masochistic relationship with the paparazzi, they in turn had a new sense of self-esteem. They no longer lived in fear and trembling before the god of newsworthiness. By the spring of 1971 they realized that the umbrella of Canadian content would protect them from the twin ravages of unemployment and inflation that had been stalking the country since the Gotterdammerung of the War Against Inflation.

By the spring of 1971 they had economic security but lacked spiritual fulfillment. They now realized that post-charisma Trudeau was determined to deprive them of the newsworthiness "stuff" that they needed to live on. Post-charisma Trudeau would give them neither charisma, nor Camelot, nor Gerda Gold. By the spring of 1971 the paparazzi, lacking the "fix" of the old sado-masochistic relationship, were suffering withdrawal symptoms. But the cure was staring them in the face; indeed, it had always been there.

It was the old marathon Dialectic Dancer stepping nimbly once again on to the dance floor as the band played "Happy Days Are Here Again." If by raising Trudeau from Lilliputian obscurity to Gulliverian heights the electronic-print paparazzi had enjoyed great highs and De Quincy delights, would not reversing the process bring equal highs and equal delights?

The paparazzi would topple the philosopher-king from his throne and that process—slow, deliberate, sometimes painful—would provide enough newsworthy "stuff," enough highs to sustain even the most hard-core paparazzi addict. By the spring of 1971 the peasant paps were ready for revolt and were beginning to beat at the very gates of the Lyceum itself with the ferocity that the oppressed always reserve for the oppressor who has lost the power to oppress.

The Philosopher-Queen Marie Antoinette

The exact beginnings of revolution are always hard to pinpoint, as any historian will be quick to tell you. But one of the more jaded members of the gallery is willing to date the beginning of the revolt of the paparazzi as that February day in 1971 when, standing at the bar of the National Press Club, gulping his fourth scotch and water, he was interrupted in his spirituous pleasures by a breathless paparazznik, one Paul Taylor of Radionews. "The prime minister," he said breathlessly, "has just told the striking Lapalme workers to 'mangez la merde' (in colloquial, unofficial English, to eat shit). Had the prime minister used the same expression to a picket demonstration by suburban youth calling for legalized marijuana, the aphorism would not only have been apt but indeed clever. (What else can you do with "shit" except smoke it or eat it?) Even in the old charisma days of "Where's Biafra?" the paps would have taken this remark as just one more example of the Trudeau wit and wouldn't even have bothered to report it.

But with the new revolutionary fervour upon them, the peasant paps were not in a friendly mood. The remark was duly reported, even though they had not heard it themselves but had only the hearsay evidence of the far-from-impartial Lapalme workers.

Well, it was fair to say that from then on, the "shit," so to speak, hit the fan. Telling striking workers, particularly Francophones, to eat shit was not then, nor ever, good politics. (The trouble with working-class picket lines is that you may find Archie Bunkers in them holding a sign.)

The Lapalme episode, if not time-wise the perfect beginning of the revolt of the paps, was certainly in the allegorical sense the classic beginning. Now the Dance of the Dialectic took a nimble pirouette. The "eat shit" remark so closely resembled Queen Marie Antoinette's famous dietary advice to the starving workers of pre-revolutionary France that it struck Duncan MacPherson like a bolt from Minerva.

Soon a nationally syndicated MacPherson cartoon depicting Trudeau in Marie Antoinette costume, fan and all, appeared in most Canadian newspapers. Trudeau, the Incorruptible Robespierre figure of the October Revolution, was now, by one of the bizarrest twists in the Dance of the Dialectic, the most notorious figure of the decadent ancien régime.

The philosopher-king had become the Philosopher-Queen Marie Antoinette. This pirouette would prove to be quite a drag on the Trudeau revolution that was supposed to provide Canadians with the permanence of Oneness and Justice. That Trudeau revolution was now beginning to devour its own children. The peasant paps had drawn first blood.

Fuddle Duddle from Peoria to Lilac

The spilling of blood continued rapidly and without surcease. Quite a lot of the royal fell in l'affaire Fuddle Duddle in March 1971. George Bain, a distinguished veteran member of the punditi-out, and a man regarded by the paparazzi with a respect and affection that bordered on the rapturous, confronted the prime minister in the government lobbies that day. In front of a pack of reporters, Mr. Bain asked him point-blank whether he, the prime minister, had told two Tory MPs in the House to "fuck off.'' Mr. Bain, whose letters from Lilac, Saskatchewan, seemed for some strange reason to convey more accurate political intelligence than the Saskatchewan desk in the PMO, was certain that "fuck off" would not play in Peoria and certainly not in Lilac; nor, for that matter, would "fuddle duddle."

Mr. Bain's irreverence in this affair and his flat refusal to buy the "fuddle duddle" explanation was not too surprising nor too hard for the Trudeau people to take. For after all, as a leading pundit-out, he had been sniping away at the king for years. What was surprising was that the prime minister left the government lobbies and Mr. Bain to face the cameras of the paparazzi and thus the eyes and ears of the nation.

There, lo and behold, CTV's Max Keeping, a distinguished veteran member of the paparazzi, screwed up his courage and asked the prime minister on air whether he had said "fuck off.'' When told "No, it was fuddle duddle,'' the subsequent laughter of the peasant paps seemed to prove that "fuddle duddle" wouldn't play on Parliament Hill, either, nor, for that matter, from Vancouver Island to Labrador. The hollow, mocking laughter of the paps seemed to one jaded observer of that particular scene to resemble the hollow laughter of Madame Lafarge as one more head bounced past her knitting basket. In the Lyceum and the concentric court circles of Rockcliffe, "fuddle duddle" played as one more flash of the royal wit. But even there, some secretly suspected that more of the purple had been shed, that the exercise of the royal wit now seemed more Nero-onic than Byronic.

Canada's Carry Nation

L'affaire Robert Muir (PC MP, Cape Breton-the Sydneys) fanned the flames of the paparazzi revolt still higher. In an exchange in the House on November 23, 1971, the post-charisma abstemious prime minister implied that the honourable member, a fourteen-year veteran of the House, was "under the influence." This, like "fuck off," was another breach of the written and unwritten rules of parliamentary etiquette. The pressures of politics, both practising it and covering it, had traditionally been soothed by the odd nip or gulp here and there of the Balm of Ginead. Traditionally too, prime ministerial complaints about the lack of sobriety in honourable members, be they in the opposition, the government backbenches or in the cabinet, were confined either to private diaries or private conversations.

Nor had the Canadian temperament ever really succumbed to the Bible-thumping rigidities of Yankee-style Prohibition. The manufacture and consumption of whiskey had always been a proud tradition of two of Canada's oldest ethnic groups, the Irish and the Scotch. A third Canadian ethnic group, the Hebrews, produced their first billionaire through the sale and manufacture of Canada's own one hundred per cent pure rye.

Even our political culture differed from the abstemious Yanks with respect to demon rum. The Father of their country *never* told a lie; the Father of our country *never* refused a drink. Even in the dull, grey, Mackenzie King-St. Laurent years, there was many a cabinet minister with his not-so-secret bar. The not-so-secret bar in the Press Gallery had been there since the Rock of Ages.

Booze had played the handmaiden to reporters of the news since the Gutenberg Galaxy first began to shine in the universe. If the prime minister were to call an honourable member a drunk and get away with it, what horrors could he and would he perpetrate on a dishonourable paparazznik, whose stupid question at a press conference might be more due to the "influence" than any basic ignorance of the fundamentals under discussion?

Needless to say, Mr. Muir was treated by the peasant paps as a martyr in this affair. The prime minister was painted as a thoughtless Yankee Bluenose, taking a verbal axe to a "por ign'rant country boy" trying his best to cope with his constituents' problems in the sinful Babylon that everyone Down East knew Ottawa to be. In another fantastic pirouette in the Dance of the Dialectic, Trudeau, the Philosopher-Queen Marie Antoinette, had become a Canadian Carry Nation.

Gray's Elegy

Shortly before the prime minister informed the paparazzi that there would be "an election-free summer," the revolt of the paps took on almost Bastille-ish overtones. Trying to recoup his losses with the peasant paps, Prime Minister Trudeau granted an exclusive interview to one of his favourite punditi-in, gruff, tough Aussie-born and bred Toronto *Star* Ottawa bureau chief, Jack Cahill. Mr. Cahill lacked the sophistication and breadth of knowledge of his Fleet Street-trained colleague Tony Westell, but his simple forthright style was certainly more easily understood by the broad masses of Ontario's Golden Horseshoe, a domain embracing roughly forty seats in the House of Commons. Using the man from down under, the PM hoped to go over the heads of the paps to allow the people once again to participate vicariously in the new Athenian democracy that was really *theirs*, not *his*.

Rhapsodizing philosophically with Mr. Cahill, the prime minister allowed that he, the PM, might *hypothetically* do something in the event that the Bourassa government might prove *hypothetically* to be "too weak" to do that which ought to be done when the events that necessitated that ought materialized.

It was another Hegelian a priori apostrophe, but the peasant paps seized on it as fresh meat for the Trudeau grinder. In the government lobbies the day the interview was published, the paps asked the prime minister if he would explain the allusion of "weak" vis-à-vis the Bourassa government.

A truculent Trudeau agreed to meet the press. He

marched down to the new headquarters of the paps in the basement of the Centre Block. He walked briskly into the small press room reserved exclusively for the Francophone division of the paparazzi. The Anglophone paps lined up dutifully with their mikes and cameras in the much larger area outside the Francophone room. This was the area designated by the Speaker and the gallery executive as their turf—the ''scrum,'' as they affectionately called it.

After approximately a half-hour wait, the prime minister and his aides emerged from the Francophone room and gleefully refused to face the Anglophone paps. ''Why don't you use the French version I've just delivered?'' he said gaily to the assembled representatives of the eyes and ears of English-speaking Canadians from the Klondike Trail to Signal Hill, as he skipped off to perform his prime ministerial duties.

The delivery of the French Connection proved abortive. When the bureau chief of one of the country's larger English TV networks informed a Trudeau press aide that he was certainly prepared to use the French version with a voice-over English translation, the Trudeau aide in question (a former paparazznik himself) blanched. He blanched in correct anticipation of the potential political havoc that would be wreaked by the prime minister addressing Anglophones not in their official language but in the other official language, the one that he had assured them time and time again they didn't need to know in order to conduct their everyday living and business. Surely listening to their prime minister speaking to them on TV at eleven o'clock in their language was part and parcel of their everyday living and business? Answering that question in the affirmative for himself, the Trudeau press aide rushed off to persuade ''Popeye'' Trudeau (now in an important cabinet committee meeting) that the French Connection had blown a fuse.

The persuading took some time. Several hours later, but still in time to beat the nationally syndicated feeds for supper-time TV, a visibly irritated Trudeau stepped into the ring with the peasant paps of Anglophonia. By now even some of the illuminati, particularly of the radical-chicci variety, had joined in for the spectacle.

Things went relatively well until the Montreal *Star*'s John Gray, generally acknowledged to be the dean emeritus of the radical chicci, briskly cut through the underbrush of paparazzi vagueness to ask the prime minister point-blank: Did he think the Bourassa government to be weak?

The prime minister, recognizing impudence when he saw it, replied to the question in the finest dialectical tradition with another question. "How's your grandmother?" the PM asked, a heavy tone of sarcasm in his voice. "She's dead," shouted the outraged Mr. Gray over the heads of the paparazzi assembled in right and left flanks beside the PM. At this juncture, the PM provided his own synthesis by turning on his heel and leaving.

It seemed to one jaded gallery observer watching this last great pre-October 1972 Trudeau confrontation with the press, that there was an element to the Trudeau-Gray slugfest that perhaps the paps missed. The element was betrayal by a member of one's own class and by a former disciple.

Mr. Gray's Toronto Rosedale aristocratic background was certainly more than equal to the prime minister's relative nouveau-richeness. Mr. Gray's scholarly accomplishments, it would be fair to say, were less spectacular than the prime minister's, but they were of a sufficient depth and range for Mr. Gray to understand what Mr. Trudeau was trying to do for the country.

After all, Mr. Gray was a former Trudeau admirer, was fluently bilingual, had lived and worked in Montreal, had been permitted access to the Lyceum, certainly knew the seriousness of the Quebec problem and, in all fairness, should have realized that the prime minister was certainly not criticizing but only speculating about Mr. Bourassa in the Cahill interview. Any other interpretation of the interview would only fan the flames of separatism, surely something neither the prime minister nor Mr. Gray, nor Mr. Gray's Westmount Outremont and Mount Royal readers really wanted to do. To the prime minister Mr. Gray's question was more cheeky than radical chicci and deserved a cheeky riposte.

The peasant paps, whose breeding and background were certainly not of the métier of either Mr. Trudeau or Mr. Gray, were in open revolt against Trudeau, the Marie Antoinette, but were not quite ready for the Girondist leadership of the radical chicci. By now they had the traditional peasant suspicion of all aristocrats, be they a Trudeau or a Danton Gray.

Still, as good revolutionary peasants, they could smell more of the purple blood in l'affaire Gray. The paps, as good peasants, shared with that class the traditional veneration of the dead. Disparaging remarks about a fellow human being's deceased grandmother (no matter how stately of origin she might have been) had grave-robberish overtones that reeked of the ghoul.

The radio and TV clip that the collective wisdom of the paps chose to illustrate that day's events with, closed with the Trudeau-Gray encounter. That night the eyes and ears of Anglophonia (equally ignorant of the basic tensions that underlay the Trudeau-Gray encounter, as were the paps) saw and heard on their home screens an angry prime minister *seemingly* berating the deceased grandmother of an obscure member of the Fourth Estate. In still another dazzling pirouette, the Dialectical Dancer had flashed one more image on the rear screen of the nation's collective subconscious. To Robespierré, Marie Antoinette and Carry Nation was now added "Alas, poor Yoricka, I knew her well!''

The peasant paps were overjoyed. They hoped that l'affaire Gray would spell elegy for post-charisma Trudeau. As for the prime minister, he failed to realize that l'affaire Gray was really only the tip of the iceberg of a spontaneous gallery conspiracy that he was willy-nilly playing Titanic to.

The very fact that the paparazzi and the radical chicci were willing to make common cause should have alarmed him just as much as the very existence of the radical chicci patently annoyed him. What annoyed Trudeau about the radical chicci was that they seemed to be the illegitimate offspring of the punditi-in. Both gallery species had endorsed him for Liberal leader and in the 1968 election. Both media species had always had easy access to the Lyceum. Both species favoured his reforms: abortion, homosexuality, divorce, prison rehabilitation, housing, drug use, tax reform, the new labour code.

Both species had been critical of the War Against Inflation, but both were willing to admit that neither the Tories nor the NDP could offer any other effective means of tackling the problem. The punditi-in stayed with Trudeau all the way on the October Crisis; the radical chicci abandoned him, after sober second thought, but were willing to live with the later Pelletier version of what, how and why it happened.

Now in the quiet warm glow of the post-charisma sunset, the radical chicci had joined the peasant paps at the storming of the gates. It made no sense. Neither did the constant ''leaking'' of ponderous government documents by angry bureaucrats and the constant printing of them by the radical chicci. Were the angry bureaucrats and the radical chicci trying to tell him something: that he wasn't activist enough; that the Lyceum was coming up with the *wrong* answers; or, worse still, not enough answers to obvious questions? Impossible! By definition it was incredible that those who should know better were saying the Brightest and the Best were the Dullest and the Worst!!

The Banditi

Still, there they were, the radical chicci in the spring of 1972, "secret" documents hot off the presses clutched in their hands, firing fusillades at Versailles itself. By now the original peasant bands of the paparazzi were fortified not only by the professional shock troops of the radical chicci and the punditi-out but also by a Quantrell guerrilla sub-species of the latter, the banditi.

The banditi—the Montreal *Gazette*'s Arthur Blakeley, FP's Vic Mackie, the Toronto *Telegram* Bureau Chief Peter Thomson, the nationally syndicated Richard Jackson of the Ottawa *Journal,* Farmer Tissington of the Thomson chain, Norman Campbell of the Ottawa *Citizen*—were conservative by nature, like the peasant paps. But, unlike the paps, they had never succumbed to Trudeaumania. Unlike the radical chicci or the punditi, in or out, they had no access to the Lyceum nor any inclination or desire for same.

The banditi were political animals out and out and real veterans of the Ottawa scene. They smelled the boredom inherent in the Permanent Trudeau Revolution early and were out to scuttle the kind before he even ascended the Liberal throne. Like the paparazzi, and unlike the radical chicci and the pundidi-out, the only good thing the banditi had to say about Trudeau was his handling of the October Crisis.

Being real political veterans and pros (some went as far back as R.B. Bennett, all as far as St. Laurent), the banditi knew what the paps and the radical chicci didn't, namely, that while the Fourth Estate can topple the king, they cannot, in a constitutional democracy, rule in his place. The banditi knew that victory could only come if Stanfield, the incredible alternative, was made the only alternative.

The Incredible Alternatives

Chapter Eight
From Forlorn Bob
to Robert Lazarus

For years, the banditi had watched the punditi-in and -out and the radical chicci playing God with the Trudeau image, turning saint into sinner and vice-versa, according to whatever whim of irony at the moment possessed them. Playing God with an epic hero like Trudeau was easy work, the cynical banditi correctly concluded. Resurrecting forlorn Stanfield and his rag-tag, bob-tail following of 1972 was something else again. This was a challenge so enormous it could fire the imagination of a Valhalla of Gods.

Slowly, painfully, and with a little help from their friends, the banditi rescued Stanfield from the political dead. Forlorn Bob was to become Robert Lazarus.

It started simply enough. As if by osmosis, the banditi persuaded the paparazzi to edit out the interminable Stanfield "pauses" from their tapes and films. A crisp new Stanfield, not quick but not slow, was presented to the eyes and ears of Anglophonia.

Again as if by osmosis, the paps, spurred on by the banditi, assigned Diefenbaker to a new role. Before the period of post-charisma Trudeau, Diefenbaker was the Tory Napoleon-in-Elba exile, the equal if not the superior of Stanfield in prestige and certainly more than Stanfield's equal in the paparazzi air time he commanded. Now Diefenbaker was assigned a more Quixotic role by the paparazzi, the comic-relief role of a W.C. Fields, whose one-liners in the defence of monarchy and at the expense of Goyer and Pelletier were gouging out gaping holes in the Trudeau windmill.

This new arrangement was tacitly accepted by all. Stanfield was restored to his proper place in the parliamentary universe as a sober, responsible leader of the opposition. Dief was back to the lone-wolf role he had played so well in the forties and fifties.

But the real winner in this new arrangement was Stanfield. Diefenbaker's baiting of the Quebec mafia would keep the West Tory, but the resentment and opprobrium of the Quebec bourgeoisie at the fierceness of this baiting would fall on Diefenbaker's shoulders, not Stanfield's. Bobby Dull, as *Le Devoir* called him, would be free to pursue the back-breaking and dull work of reviving Tory fortunes in Quebec, doing the Lazarus work there that the banditi had done for him on Parliament Hill.

But Robert Lazarus had more tricks up his sleeve. Shortly after the October Crisis, one of the fastest verbal guns in Canada's Wild West, a veritable Will Rogers, joined the Stanfield camp. The previously subdued wit of Forlorn Bob and the exuberant irrepressible wit of Bill Grogan were to spin an invisible lariat that would rope in even the most skeptical members of the gallery illuminati.

The first joint Stanfield-Grogan effort was the 1971 Press Gallery dinner. (This dinner, interestingly enough, was held just a few weeks after Trudeau's secret marriage, an event that, if not chronologically, at least allegorically ushered in the post-charisma phase of Trudeau politics.) At that 1971 dinner the astonished assembled press illuminati from the gallery and across the country and the equally astonished politicians and mandarins heard the dry, laconic, Lincolnesque figure stringing Leacockian one-liners into hilarious pearls of wisdom.

Trudeau's performance at this all-important annual event was dismal. He was not at his best and he was certainly not happy. In dismay he watched Stanfield, the long-distance runner, beating the Trudeau Road Runner to the punchline every time. Indeed, at that event, even the speech of Pierre O'Neill, the gallery president (liberally ghost-written by the mysterious Jaded Observer, a college classmate of Whipper Billy Grogan) was considered to be far superior to that of the prime minister. Now even the punditi-in were prepared to admit that Stanfield had at least as good a sense of humour as the increasingly petulant Pierre.

That 1971 gallery dinner, closed to the eyes and ears of the nation, was, if not historically at least allegorically, the coming to life of Lazarus Bob. It followed as night follows day that if Stanfield was as *witty* as Trudeau, it was hypothetically possible that he was as *bright* as Trudeau. At least Stanfield's one-liners could be understood by all the members of the gallery, from the loftiest punditi-in to the lowliest paparazznik.

As for post-charisma Trudeau, his 1972 gallery speech was even worse than the year before; Stanfield's even better. In post-charisma Trudeauland prime ministerial references to Montesquieu, Acton or Aristophanes no longer caused a loving Gallery Gold Rush to the Parliamentary Library to find out what the references meant. Now they simply elicited a collective gallery yawn, the yawn reserved for a bore.

Lazarus Bob had one still more devastating trick up his sleeve. In post-charisma Trudeauland he was displaying an uncanny Mackenzie Kingish ability to straddle the centre position, a position which Trudeau, for some bizarre reason, seemed to be vacating. Not only was Stanfield's ability to go for the jugular centre Mackenzie Kingish, but in style and technique he was Kingish as well. Both men were renowned for their patience and stamina. Both used self-deprecation as effective political techniques. King always played the humble Uriah Heep;

Stanfield preferred the humble Honest Abe. King used a torrent of circuitous phrases to camouflage his true intent; Stanfield, the quasi-Mackenzie King, used very few words delivered very slowly to hide his true intent. And both men would agree that a decision *not* taken today causes far less political harm tomorrow than a wrong decision taken today which you're stuck with tomorrow.

Even in the Trudeau charisma days, Stanfield seemed to know when the tortoise should keep his head in his shell and, more important, when to poke it out. In the October Crisis, he got neither the glory of the NDP's defence of the "bleeding hearts" and the "weak-kneed" nor Trudeau's glory of being the first prime minister since Mackenzie King in 1939 to stand up to the excesses of Quebec nationalism. Stanfield got neither the glory reaped by either side nor the opprobrium heaped on both. The Stanfield position of "War Measures if necessary but not necessarily War Measures" was one he could honourably rest his oars on.

In the great tax-reform debate, Stanfield picked up all the brownie points. In no way was he tinged with the extremism of the Canadian Council for Fair Taxation but that Poujadist-Babbitt vote would nevertheless by default be as much his as the anti-Pelletier-Goyer vote in monarchy- and RCMP-loving rural Anglophonia. Stanfield also picked up all the votes of those less greedy and more needy citizens who agreed with him that neither the family home nor the family farm should be subject to capital gains tax. This political windfall came to him because the superconfident Trudeau forces preferred administrative symmetry to political reality. A buck is a buck, but the buck should stop at the farm gate and the door of the family dwelling, Stanfield argued slowly but well.

Now another political windfall came his way and Stanfield made the most of it. Nixonomics struck at Canada in August 1971; in one fell swoop it brought an end to that good old Expo feeling of cockiness and arrogance Canadians had been feeling since the mid sixties. Nixonomics reinforced the fears and doubts that had been steadily plaguing Canadians since the War Against Inflation had failed to stop either price increases or the high numbers of unemployed who were the war's inevitable casualties. To make the situation even worse, Nixonomics came at a time when Britain, our Motherland and one of our biggest markets, was joining the European Economic Community, leaving us alone in North America with Uncle Sam.

Trudeau had described that continental relationship as a mouse sleeping with an elephant: "Every twitch and groan of the latter made the former nervous." Nixonomics, with its surcharges and DISC plans, was making Canadians feel mousy, twitchy, nervous. The surcharges and the DISC seemed to imply that our branchplant economy would be stomped out of existence by the Republican elephants of San Clemente.

We were no longer to enjoy Yankee affluence without Yankee responsibilities. In the new Nixon order of things we were to have neither affluence nor responsibility—just wood to hew and water to draw. The process smacked of Lenin's definition of imperialism, the prime minister informed a startled Charles Lynch.

What neither Charles Lynch nor Mr. Trudeau were talking about was where the action lay, in the traditional ambivalence with which the Canadian collective subconscious came to grips with big old nasty Uncle Sam. That traditional ambivalence was a contradictory mixture of love and hate, a Quixotic desire to tilt at Yankee windmills, yet a fear and trembling in the presence of the awesome God of American Capitalism. The Liberals, the party of nineteenth century reason and logic, free trade and internationalism, were traditionally best at dealing with Uncle Sam when he was a Good Neighbour. The

Tory party, crotchetly anti-American and nationalist in the British-connection sense, but as a good business party just as respectful of Yankee ingenuity as anyone else, was the party that traditionally reaped the harvest when Uncle Sam turned nasty.

What Tories were always good at was exploiting both the love-hatred and awe-fear that the mouse feels for the elephant. Thus, when Good Neighbour Taft offered us reciprocity in 1911, the Tories could, at one and the same time, yell "no truck nor trade with the Yankees" while contending that a strong, protective tariff was good for Canada because it forced these same Yankees to build their branchplants here, creating truck-and-trade jobs for Canadians. The Tories won that one. When Uncle Sam turned Smoot-Hawley-ish (the highest American tariff in history) in 1930, Canadians turned to R.B. Bennett. He promised to "blast his way" into world markets and particularly the American one by matching the Yankee tariff wall brick for brick. Economically, these Tory positions made no sense. Psychologically, they satisfied the Canadian ambivalence and politically they seemed to work.

Given Nixonomics and the quietude of Francophonia, Canadians seemed to be calling for leaders whose expertise was not in Quebec but in the dynamics of North American capitalism. These leaders, the Canadian subconscious Jung-ery insisted, should have the tough WASP ability to play economic poker with the shrewd WASP, Tricky Dicky. In the immediate wake of Nixonomics, Bill Davis swept to power in Ontario. The victory seemed to reflect the belief of branchplant-dependent Ontari-ari-ari-o-ans that quiet shrewd WASP bad-on-TV Bill could better handle quiet, shrewd WASP bad-on-TV Tricky Dicky than either rustic Bob Nixon or one hundred per cent-pure Yankee-hating socialist Stephen.

On the national scene, Canadians began to ask them-

selves these questions: Is Trudeau the philosopher-king,
the Hegelian man of Ideas, *necessarily* the best man to
deal in this crass, materialist world with crass, materialist
Uncle Sam? Wasn't slow-talking, bad-on-TV Bob Stanfield the combo image of Honest Abe Lincoln and Nova
Scotia's Sam Slick? Wasn't he in essence the honest,
shrewd Yankee trader and therefore not *necessarily* the
worst man to deal in this crass materialist world with crass,
materialist, bad-on-TV Tricky Dicky?

Wasn't it also true, as the paps were only too quick
to point out, that on his visit to Washington, Stanfield
was received warmly while the great pre-Watergate Nixon
seemed to show only coldness for Pierre? (Not to mention
the motherly condescension the paps said Pat was supposed to have shown Margaret, one year junior to Julie and
three years junior to Trish.)

The answers English Canadians were giving to these
questions were a major breakthrough for Bob Stanfield.
By the summer of 1972, it would be fair to say that an
overwhelming majority of Anglophonia still believed Trudeau was the best man and the Liberals the best party
to handle a Quebec crisis. By the fall of 1972 Trudeau
had pronounced the land to be strong and Quebec no problem. From then on, it would be fair to say that a majority
of Anglophonia felt the best man and the best party to
handle the economy and Uncle Sam was Lazarus Bob
and the Tory party. What mousy, twitchy, nervous Anglophonia seemed now to be asking for was the stamina and
caution of the quasi-Mackenzie King-ish Bob Stanfield
rather than the strident Meighen confidence of the unrevised and unrepentant Pierre Elliott Trudeau.

Chapter Nine
Lewis:
From David to Goliath
and Back Again

Perhaps a more accurate assessment of the mousy mood of Anglophonia in the fall of 1972 would be to say that the overwhelming majority of its citizens felt the Trudeau Lyceum was not the best mechanism to handle the economy or Uncle Sam. For by the summer of 1972, little David, Sophie and all the Lewises were getting their feet wet in the Trudeau-baiting act. Joining Stanfield, the peasant paps, the radical chicci, the punditi-out and the banditi, the Lewises were contributing their considerable talents to the new Anglophonia "All in the Family" game, the converting of the Lyceum into a Berlin Bunker.

That the NDP and the Lewises should be alive and well in the summer of 1972 was to some extent the by-product of the political universe unfolding as it should. To some extent it was also due to the political ineptitude and tunnel vision of the Trudeaucrats. For had Trudeau been Mackenzie King, rather than a philosopher-king, the NDP might have vanished into the Great Beyond, reachable only by a medium's crystal ball.

Despite the Hartzian "fragment" theories of Gad Horowitz, there was no historical inevitability about the continued existence of socialism on Canadian soil; no more historical inevitability than, say, the continued existence of liberalism on British soil. In politics materialists make history, not the Hegelian vice-versa. To paraphrase Plekhanov ruthlessly, Napoleon made history; there was no necessity to invent him.

These lessons of history were well understood by both Mackenzie King and one of his self-proclaimed admirers, John G. Diefenbaker. Both the small-l liberal and the populist knew that if you want to occupy the centre and hold it, you must annihilate the opposition flank to the left.

Old wily Willy always did it with kindness and courtesy and by clever shifts to the left. In 1935 the CCF had seven federal seats; in 1940 eight and in his last election, 1945, they rose to twenty-eight, eighteen of those from Saskatchewan which the year before had turfed out a corrupt Liberal Gardiner machine and replaced it with the Baptist purity of T.C. Douglas. But not a seat for the CCF in Ontario, which two years before had come within a hair's breadth of a CCF provincial government. Unemployment insurance, family and veterans' allowances, had given King the Roosevelt-New Deal image which was more than enough to keep CCF social democracy in its place where it counted, in the country's industrial heartland—Ontario.

What King smothered with kindness, Dief the Populist smote with battle axe and bludgeon. In 1958 the Great Commoner not only swept social democracy off the Great Plains but did victorious battle with it in the very heart of its proletarian base. In 1958 the two seats of Winnipeg North, the Bethlehem of Canadian socialism, went Conservative. So did the working-class areas of every major city in Anglophonia. As of 1958, Woodsworth's Co-operative Commonwealth was as extinct as the dodo.

The one man who refused to give up the good fight was David Lewis. Out of the ashes of the CCF, he was determined to revive Canadian socialism and build a New Party. This new party was not to be modelled, as was Woodsworth's, on Norman Thomas's Co-operative Commonwealth, but hopefully on the more successful New Deal-Democratic party that usurped and swept the

Thomas socialists aside.

Tommy Douglas's government still remained intact in Saskatchewan; the CCF still held on to the working-class seats of Winnipeg in the Manitoba legislature and the CCF was still the official opposition in BC. What Dief had done federally, he had not done provincially. The renegade was too preoccupied with holding power in Imperial Rome to worry about the pesky provinces.

To this farmer-working-stiff base, Lewis was determined to add a third ingredient, one that Woodsworth had never bothered with and Roosevelt always had—the progressive, right-thinking and mobile middle and upper-middle classes and those sons of farmers and workers who were rapidly entering them as a result of the fluid affluent, post-war dynamics of the 1950s.

As Diefenbaker began to decay in power, the New Party, now interestingly enough calling itself the New Democratic Party (a clever contraction of Roosevelt's New Deal-Democratic party), found itself having to compete briskly and not too successfully with the new left-wing Liberalism of Lester Pearson for the right-thinking urban upper and middle classes. It was doing better with the workers. The NDP carried BC in the 1962, '63 and '65 federal elections, regained its old base in Winnipeg and clung to its old turf in northern Ontario. It made no dent in Diefenbaker's farm support but was picking up the odd urban seat in Ontario, like middle-class branch-plant Peterborough, for example.

Then along came Plaza Pierre. In 1968 he completely annihilated the NDP's middle- and upper-middle-class base. But he failed to do what King and Diefenbaker did before him, i.e., destroy the socialists in their rural-populist and urban-proletariat lairs. In 1968 Pierre triumphantly toured the shopping plazas that Pearson had already carried before him. The Trudeau motorcade did not turn left to the working-class and factory areas of urban Anglophonia (as

John Munro and Bryce Mackasey had been frantically urging). There working-class wives were deserting the NDP in droves (as many an NDP canvasser was willing to testify), but they and their husbands waited in vain for the Trudeaucade to show up. In the Toronto area the NDP clung to their labour base in York South, Broadview, Greenwood and Oshawa-Whitby. In Winnipeg they carried three of the city's five seats. In BC they held on in Vancouver and were second to the victorious Trudeau in the province as a whole.

What was even more bizarre, Trudeau's popularity with the western farmers he liked to helicopter-visit was simply eating into the old Diefenbaker base. In 1968 the Liberal vote in Saskatchewan went up high enough for the NDP to carry the province for the first time since 1957. Trudeau the philosopher-king was no Mackenzie King; the NDP had survived to live and fight another day.

1969 looked like the end of the beginning when Ed Schreyer swept to power in Manitoba. Schreyer, who openly confessed to a jaded CBC interviewer that his view of social democracy was on a par with Roosevelt's New Deal, did, in Manitoba-miniature, what Lewis dreamt of nationally. Schreyer had carried the city labour vote, the province's rural vote and a very considerable slice of Manitoba's right-thinking upper and middle classes.

But alack, alas, as fall followed summer, 1969 began to look like the beginning of the end. What Trudeau had failed to do to Lewis, the Waffle seemed to accomplish effortlessly. Their strident cry for Quebec self-determination and the nationalization of "the commanding heights of the economy" were plunging the Lewisites into the political lower depths. The Waffle mastery of socialist in-fighting, namely mike-control, delegate discipline and *zitsfleisch* (the ability to sit on your ass in a hot convention hall until hell freezes over and your opposition gets bored and leaves) were making a mockery out of the Lewis family's vaunted political cunning. Given the traditional socialist belief in openness and faith in the public, the TV cameras and mikes were everywhere. The public disembowelling of the NDP was soon to become one of Anglophonia's favourite spectator sports.

In the spring of 1971, Lewis had to endure the humiliating TV spectacle of a fight-to-the-finish with a mere post-war baby stripling for the leadership of a party he had himself founded. In that NDP convention, Jim Laxer was the Waffle David who almost knocked the bloated Goliath of Canadian socialism off his very wobbly feet. (The Lewis victory celebration was the quietest one that the Jaded Observer could recall in over a decade of covering these peculiar rites. The Lewis quest for revenge seen by that same Jaded Observer in a quiet tête-à-tête with the Lewis family that evening was certainly one of the bloodthirstiest his collective memory, conscious or unconscious, could recall.)

But once again the Dialectic trotted on to the marathon dance floor and did one more nimble pirouette. Bloodied Goliath was to become lean and hungry David once again. True, some blood-letting continued for quite some time and particularly in Ontario, but somehow the blood-letting seemed to have some curative effects.

In late June 1971, shortly after the Lewis convention débâcle, the NDP rode to an overwhelming triumph in Saskatchewan. They had taken forty-five of the sixty seats and fifty-five per cent of the popular vote in an election where the Waffle was the major target of the incumbent Liberals. The farmer, the worker, the sophisticated academic-professional of Saskatoon and Regina, the WASP and the ethnic had given the Lewis New Deal dream still another victory in the new, more urbanized, more affluent homeland of the Regina Manifesto.

The Ontario election was a blow, but really not a mortal

one. Nixonomics and the Red Tory-Davis image of Dalton Camp's Stop Spadina did far more to explain the dimensions of non-NDP growth than the supposed bloodletting of the Waffle.

But the real acid test was the stunning Barrett victory in the summer of 1972. Barrett, the Jew, and an original sponsor of the Waffle Manifesto, had pulled the biggest coup of all—a New Deal-coalition victory in lunchpail Lotusland. What was particularly interesting was that Barrett had done so with the full cooperation and good behaviour of both the Lotusland Wafflers and Lunchpailers acting under the campaign directorship of one Hans Brown. (Mr. Brown, a former aide to T.C. Douglas, was a bitter anti-Lewis Waffler at the 1971 leadership convention.)

What Barrett proved to anyone but the most resolute skeptic was that the NDP House was no longer divided against itself; it was now a political home for thousands of Canadians from the Ontario border to the Pacific slopes. Pierre Elliott Trudeau had once argued that the proper road to a Socialist Rome lay through the provinces. Now three of them were in socialist hands. Could Rome be far away?

The Trudeau Lyceum seemed unimpressed. As one Trudeaucrat put it to the Jaded Observer that summer, there was little, if any, correlation between provincial and federal voting patterns. The Jaded Observer, reflecting on a country with three NDP provincial fiefdoms, four Tory ones and only three Liberal, wondered aloud whether these compartments were as watertight as the Lyceum suggested. He wondered even more when he considered that of the seven federal by-elections held in Anglophonia since 1968, five had gone NDP, two Conservative; in six of them the victory margins ranged from the enormous to the very comfortable.

What the Trudeaucrats had failed or refused to notice,

the punditi-out and the radical chicci were only too glad
to recognize. Unlike the banditi, their motto was—*any*
alternative to Trudeau was credible and desirable. The
pundit-out Doug Fisher, whose relationship with David
Lewis was not always cordial but whose loathing of the
Waffle was legendary, began to praise Lewis in his
Toronto *Sun* columns. Lubor Zink, the ultra-conservative
pundit-out, continuously complimented Lewis for his
purge of the ultra-ultra Wafflers. George Bain's Letters
from Lilac reflected general good tidings about the new
socialist dispensation in Saskatchewan and if George continued to be crotchety with all politicians, he was now
less crotchety with Lewis than he had been for some time.

But the ultimate coup de grâce came from the "Poor
man's Scotty Reston," Charles Lynch of the Southam
News Service. In surely one of the more dazzling
pirouettes in the Dance of the Dialectic, Charles, whose
favorite pastime was previewing the Press Gallery show,
songs, harmonica and all, for Buck Crump, President of
the CPR, was now in his columns praising David Lewis
as the greatest thing to hit the Ottawa White Way since
Mom and apple pie.

This event was a momentous one. What Lewis knew
and the Lyceum didn't seem to was that the beauty of
being a poor man's anything is this: since there are more
poor men than rich, there are more readers of Lynch's
gay, "lightweight" (to quote *Maclean's*) prose than rich
readers of the more heady stuff of the punditi-in. If there
are more readers in Lynchland than in Westell-Desbarats
turf, might there not be more voters there too? The answer
was obvious.

Equally obvious was that this Lewis endorsement was
the final Lynch-pin in the grand alliance of paparazzi,
radical chicci, banditi and punditi-out. History, said Lord
Acton, was a hanging judge. Now, waiting anxiously outside the Lyceum gates, was Hanging Judge Charlie and

the gallery's Lynching Bee.

The political-science lessons the banditi had taught earlier had now been learnt. Trudeau the philosopher-king could now be strung up because now there were two credible alternatives to take his place—Forlorn Bob, now Robert Lazarus, and Goliath Lewis, now Sling-Shot Dave.

Messages for the Emperor

Chapter Ten
The Messengers:
All Quiet on the Lyceum Front

What was astonishing to more than one jaded observer
that summer of '72 was the relative peace and calm that
emanated from the East Block Lyceum. One could scarce-
ly hear the blood-curdling Apache war cries of the gallery
as they circled round and round the Trudeau covered
wagons.

By now Kierans and Givens had abandoned ship. Hellyer, Ryan and Rock did what was hitherto unheard of
in modern-day Liberalism: they not only abandoned ship
but swam to warm and welcome Tory shores. Still not
a murmur or a peep out of the East Block. All quiet too
on the Lyceum front when Romeo LeBlanc departed for
the Groves of Acadian Academe. M. LeBlanc, former
press secretary to Pearson and Trudeau, certainly heard
the gallery war cries. To the sensitive, they could be heard
as far away as Moncton.

M. LeBlanc, a former paparazznik and pundit himself,
knew his gallery well. His relationship with the press was
not exactly Romeo and Juliet but neither was it Montague
and Capulet. M. LeBlanc was of the Clyde Beatty school.
Gallery lions need to be fed huge chunks of meat and
gently whipped if they are to be kept happy and in line.
To deal with the lions of the gallery you've got to get
into the cage with them and get your hands dirty in the
process.

M. LeBlanc's replacement was a diplomat, and neither

lions nor Apaches take kindly to diplomats. They prefer the jungle frontier diet of the last man at the last post to the canapés and cocktails of Emily Post.

P.M. Roberts, the new press secretary, was, like his Broadway-play namesake, an intellectual, decent and honourable man. He naturally preferred the company of intellectual, decent and honourable men. That the punditi-in certainly were, one and all. From them he tried to learn what the lesser breeds in the gallery were up to, but the punditi-in were now too immersed in the dazzling court life of Versailles to see and appreciate the shadows of rebellion flickering by on the plebian walls of the Parliamentary Press Gallery.

In the inner marrow of his bones, Mr. Roberts, a good diplomat, like Mr. Pearson and Citizen Talleyrand before him, sensed the Great Trouble that lay ahead. But, like Mr. Pearson, he was either unwilling to fight what Fate had seemingly decreed, or, like Mr. Talleyrand, refused to be the emperor's messenger. Imperial messengers, after all, can only tell the emperor there is no more time and any more efforts would be too little or too late.

Certainly, by the summer of 1972, there were certain messages the prime minister should have been getting loud and clear, messenger or no messenger. The Kierans departure indicated a revolutionary restlessness within the bowels of the Lyceum itself. The departure of Hellyer, Givens and Ryan, three of Toronto's most important life-long Liberals, indicated enormous discontent within the Liberal organization in a province that had delivered 64 seats in 1968.

As for the Charles Lynching Bee outside the Lyceum, the members of it weren't exactly the Invisible Hordes of the Apocalypse. By the summer of 1972, three of its Horsemen had given full, visible evidence of the gallery conspiracy. Peter Reilly, a venerable paparazznik, and that species' most virulent Trudeau-hater, had won the nomination in Ottawa West at a monster rally in which two of the four thousand delegates cheering Reilly were the veteran banditi Richard Jackson of the Ottawa *Journal* and Norman Campbell of the Ottawa *Citizen*. Lubor Zink, the multicultural king of the punditi-out, was the declared Conservative candidate against "What's up, Doc" Haidasz in Toronto Parkdale. Soon to join Reilly in another open display of paparazzi revolt was CTV's Max Keeping (he of "fuck off" question fame), who was prepared to kamikaze Don Jamieson in his Burin-Burgeo Newfie stronghold.

Seemingly there was no need for an emperor's messenger, for the handwriting loomed large on the Lyceum wall. The question was, how many mene menes does it take to tickle-tekel a Trudeau parson out of his self-complacent lethargy?

Chapter Eleven
Canada First, Trudeau Last

The answer to the afore-mentioned question seemed, in the summer of 1972, to be a helluva lot of tickle-tekels. One message the emperor was clearly not receiving was this: the temperature reading for Canadian nationalism (Anglophonia-style) was not medium-cool but feverishly hot.

The Lyceum's misreading of the political significance of the new nationalism in Anglophonia was in part due to Trudeau's lifelong distaste for nationalism of any kind. The zenophobic and racist qualities that displayed themselves in the nationalism of Francophonia he was certain would equally show up in the new nationalism of Anglophonia. In this analysis Trudeau was enthusiastically supported by Professor Ramsay Cook, his Boswell and his eyes and ears into the cultural élite of Anglophonia.

(Professor Cook knew his Anglophone nationalists well. The Jaded Observer first met Professor Cook when they were both students at Winnipeg's United College in the early fifties. The former, an uncouth slum urchin and one-time highschool failure and university-expellee, had recovered his fortunes somewhat. There the Jaded Observer heard the brilliant and precocious Ramsay Cook deliver a superb paper on something the North-Dead-End Kid had never heard of before, a political movement called Canada First. At that particular moment, the Kid only half digested what the brilliant, older and wiser Jake was saying. Years later he was to discover that the Canada Firsters were Francophonia Lasters. They were French-hating Anglo-Saxon bigots determined to make Canada the number one jewel in the imperial crown. In their Canada, Britannia would rule and Francophonia would be its dutiful and obedient subject or else.)

Professor Cook was quick to spot the far less virulent but potential zenophobia seemingly inherent in the laments for the Anglo-Canadian alliance and the British connection that the Jeremiads of George Grant and Donald Creighton *seemed* to convey. In the Toronto *Star*-Walter Gordon school of nationalism Professor Cook could see only the Old Ontario centralism rearing its ugly head once again to colonize the Maritimes, Quebec and the West.

As for the pan-Canadian socialist-nationalism of the dynamic Hebrew Trinity of Professors Gad Horowitz, Cy Gonick and Jim Laxer, why that was the absurdest nationalist form of all. Professor Cook deliciously called it the Canadian National Liberation Front. All the confirmation of the absurdity of the latter group that was necessary in the Cook view was simply to watch their quasi-hysterical Waffle pyrotechnics at the NDP conventions of 1969 and 1971.

What Trudeau and Cook were offering in place of these new ghetto absurdities were the patriotic pleasures of the nation-state rather than the patent excesses of the nationalist state. But if intellectually the Cook's tour of the new nationalism of Anglophonia was a veritable guru's gourmet delight, in the realm of political reality Cook's ideas were completely half-baked.

What he and the Lyceum failed to ask themselves were these two very important political questions. Why were important sections of all three major parties of Anglophonia embracing the new nationalism? If the Waffle was the Canadian National Liberation Front, then *who* was Canada's Generalissimo Ky?

An intelligent answer to the first question was staring Cook and the Trudeau Lyceum in the face. What was interesting about the Waffle was that they were all young, bright, well-educated and the sons and daughters of Anglophonia's upper and middle classes. The most stridently socialist and nationalist Waffle resolutions at NDP conventions came from such NDP constituency associations as Toronto Rosedale, Kingston (Queen's University), Saskatoon (University of Saskatchewan), Winnipeg South (the Wellington Crescent turf of James Richardson) and Vancouver South (the turf of the Hon. Arthur Laing).

The Waffle was not the by-product of the teeming huddled masses of Woodsworthia. They were salon-socialists-nationalists with a vengeance. For any shrewd Trudeaucrat who cared to peek beyond the rubble the Waffle left behind them at NDP conventions, these Waffle kids bore a striking physical and cultural resemblance to the sons and daughters of upper- and middle-class Anglophonia who shouted their hearts out for Trudeau in the Liberal convention of 1968.

That convention conjures up, of course, the Liberal Trinity of Walter Gordon, Pauline Jewett and Mel Hurtig, who fought and bled for the Trudeau nomination against the wicked continentalism of Hellyer-Winters. By the summer of 1972, if not Ramsay Cook, at least some observant Trudeaucrats should have wondered why the Toronto *Star*'s Walter Gordon and Beland Honderich were daily saying "Up periscope!" and firing one torpedo after another at the "weak-kneed" Gray bill on foreign ownership (to the point of the *Star* ultimately endorsing for the first time in its history the Conservative Party of Canada); why Mel Hurtig in the wilds of Edmonton of all places was bitterly attacking Trudeau's energy and foreign-ownership policy; and why Pauline Jewett, a lifelong Liberal, should quit the party to run for the NDP.

Surely the Trudeaucrats should have been puzzled by the fact that Walter Gordon's chief disciple was Melville Watkins, now playing the Waffle's gentile Lenin to Laxer's Jewish Trotsky. If that strange link didn't pique their curiosity, then how about the Tory party's Fast Eddie Goodman and Florid Flora MacDonald playing camp followers, this time not to Dalton, but to the Red Tory theories of Gad Horowitz.

Surely one thing was clear: the new nationalism of Anglophonia may have been the frail intellectual reed Professor Cook had labelled it, but a very considerable portion of the upper and middle classes were clinging to it. What was equally ominous was that among the fish loose in this new sea of nationalism were former Trudeau enthusiasts and killer whales like Peter Newman, Robert Fulford and historians Pierre Berton and William Kilbourn.

It was these classes and this intelligentsia that had done as much or more than the paparazzi to bring Trudeau the keys to the Peaceable Kingdom. Now, in another fantastic pirouette in the Dance of the Dialectic, the Right Honourable Pierre Elliott Trudeau had become Canada's Generalissimo Ky. Now the Canadian National Liberation Front (Creighton - Grant - Goodman - Hurtig - Jewett - Gordon - Honderich - Watkins - Laxer - Horowitz - Berton - Newman - Fulford - Kilbourn) were daily lobbing artillery shells into the very inner sancta of Trudeau Tara, soon to become—Saigon with the Wind.

Conversations with Canadians

Chapter Twelve
The Odd Couple:
The Jaded Observer in Happy and Unhappy Colloquy with the Friendly Trudeaucrat

On Friday, September 1, 1972, the Right Honourable Pierre Elliott Trudeau, clutching his Socratic Academy Award in his hand, skipped nimbly out of the Centre Block, west entrance, and into his limousine for a quick trip to Rideau Hall. There the Governor General was informed that "the election-free summer" had come to an end. The Canadian public, millions of whom were on the highways heading for a Labour Day weekend, were informed via a TV press conference special that their chance to applaud and ratify four years of Lyceum good works had now arrived.

For the Jaded Observer this was his first chance to see a Parliament dissolve and he was called in to help preside over the final electronic rites for the 28th Parliament. On air he noted wistfully that the prime minister was calling for a new mandate on the basis of great things accomplished in the past, but wondered why the prime minister, in his quest for a summer-vacation holiday, had allowed the Family Income Security Plan, the Gray bill on foreign ownership and the new Industrial Strategy inherent in the Turner corporate tax cuts to languish in parliamentary limbo. Did the failure to have these programs enacted into law before a summer recess and an intervening election mean that the prime minister didn't consider these bills important, the Jaded Observer asked himself quietly? Or did it mean that victory was so certain that the prime minister could clean up these loose ends in a quick post-victory session in the fall?

These questions bothered the Jaded Observer only for a moment. His interest was quickly absorbed by the prime minister's press conference and the penetrating question of pundit-in Peter Desbarats of the Toronto *Star* as to whether Margaret or Justin would be involved in the campaign.

The PM's negative reply elicited an odd, hushed, negative response from the disappointed paps, but the atmosphere in the conference room was genial, cheery and confident. It was as if the PM's obvious self-confidence had spilled over on to his gallery enemies.

Trudeau's obvious belief that a quick and easy victory was at hand made many of the illuminati and paparazzi hesitate. Maybe they were wrong, after all. Maybe Robert Lazarus was really Forlorn Bob and Lewis more Goliath than David. If these two were still incredible alternatives, it struck many a pundit and a paparazznik that four more years of fighting a victorious philosopher-king would for them be an equally incredible alternative. Perhaps it was time to go from punditi-out and radical chicci to punditi-in and from post-charisma revolutionary peasant paps to acquiescent pleasant paps. Maybe the Trudeau "peace in our time" was for all time, and one just had to get used to it.

Or maybe the Trudeau "peace in our time" was a Chamberlain piece of paper waving in the air, easily blown over by the gusty storm just over the horizon. The Jaded Observer knew the answer to that question would come on the campaign trail and in the "Conversations with Canadians" the prime minister proposed as his campaign Weltanschauung. The answer, he was certain, would not come from the back-seat view of a paparazzi seat in the PM's campaign jet.

On-the-spot observance of an election campaign, the

Jaded Observer knew, was not necessarily the best way to find out what's happening. He had covered many elections, federal and provincial. He guessed right in 1965, wrong in 1968. (He bet on a Trudeau minority government, the schmuck!) Provincially he guessed right in Manitoba in '66 and '69; right in Nova Scotia in '67, wrong in '70; dead on in Ontario and in Alberta in '71; dead on in Quebec in '70 on unfamiliar turf; dead wrong in BC in '72 on unfamiliar turf which he did not cover but which friends in the know told him about but he would not listen; but not dead wrong on his prediction that the Barrett provincial victory would have devastating spillovers on any federal election to follow. It was a political-forecast track record that hardly rivalled that of Jim Thorpe or Mackenzie King's crystal ball, but one that did compare favourably with the prognostications of a Marie Antoinette, a Nicholas Alexandra and a Neville Chamberlain.

The Jaded Observer was a strange man. Physically he was of Hitchcockian proportions but his accomplishments, it would be fair to say, were far less spectacular. Still, like Hitchcock, he was in the film business in a loose sort of sense and, like Hitchcock, he liked hiding himself in a Hampstead maze of his own concoction. There was also a certain air of desperation about him for he was blessed or cursed by the ownership of a magical false nose and glasses magical in that the glasses came off but the nose didn't.

The Jaded Observer was to be described in a Halifax *Chronicle Herald* editorial as "nauseating," "crude," "rude" and yet, O wonders of the Dialectic, as "a brilliant—almost too brilliant—political analyst." The Toronto *Star*'s Anthony Westell, dean of the punditi-in, viewed him as "the Press Gallery's resident wit" and "a student of political history." The *Globe and Mail*'s Dennis Braithwaite once called him "Canada's Mort

Sahl''; *Saturday Night*'s Robert Fulford had once called him "a boor."

Fulford's *Saturday Night* colleague Mary Lowrey Ross chose to refer to the Jaded Observer as "an anonymous sensitive interviewer." The *Telegram*'s Merle Shain felt he was a "Thing," while *Maclean's* Heather Robertson, feeling around the inner private parts of his on-camera soul, pronounced him a "castrate." (In post-October Trudeauland, she would upgrade him to "wonderful.")

Anonymous phone callers in the middle of the night were less kind to the Jaded Observer than his press colleagues. They called him everything from a "Jewish Nazi" (a contradiction in terms he couldn't understand) to a "male chauvinist pig" (which his castrata status made a biological impossibility.) "Drunk," "stupid," "obnoxious" were other adjectives employed by the anonymati.

Rabbis had denounced the Jaded Observer in the pulpit. A Westmount resident he once paid a visit to, with a group of film friends, tried to cane him to death. (The Jaded Observer always fondly referred to that episode as his Citizen Cane epic.) And a group of Winnipeggers of native extraction once threatened to scalp him.

Still, there were some consolations. One anonymous phone caller would insist that he would "vote" for the Jaded Observer and would also insist that he "be given a Gold Star of David" for his general good works. A piece the Jaded Observer had once written was published in Winnipeg's *Israelite Press*. United Church ministers and the Law Society of Alberta invited him to address their parsonages. He had once been the guest speaker at the conventions of the Royal Canadian Institute of Architects, the BC Association of Architects and the United Steelworkers of America (Canadian section).

Frankly, the Jaded Observer was dismayed and at times downright terrified at the fuss his behaviour seemed to stir up. This Jaded Castrata was no Norman Mailer, rough, tough and ready; this one was really an "electronic ant-eater" and a "chicken-hearted Trotsky," as he had often described himself to his listeners and readers.

Philosophically, his home environment was historical materialism. In college, only vaguely remembering that Marx had stood Hegel on his head, he had great difficulty in understanding Plato, Aristotle, Kant and Hegel, i.e., how to stand Karl Marx on his head without getting intellectually dizzy in the process. In college, he met his first Liberal and his first Progressive Conservative; in his childhood he had known only CCFers and Communists. (Liberals and Conservatives, his mother told him, visited the neighbourhood only on Christmas and on election day, but they always brought food baskets.)

In his maturity and male menopause he was terrified to find that at many a chichi Ottawa cocktail party he was attacked by his betters for not being radical or socialist enough; or even worse, was accused of exaggerating the dimensions of his "deprived" background. One beautiful and talented Rockcliffe matron even informed him that she had visited his old Winnipeg neighbourhood and that the houses looked "real nice." So "obsequious" was the Jaded Observer that he failed to inform his accuser that his old neighbourhood had undergone a bit of a townhouse resurgence, like Toronto's Cabbagetown, now listed as a choice location in the *Globe and Mail*'s realty pages. The obsequious Jaded Observer only wondered quietly to himself how the beautiful Rockcliffe belle would have handled Hugh Garner in a similar cocktail party Dialectic.

But worst of all, the Jaded Observer was compulsively indecisive and a compulsive member of the cult of the political personality. He liked politicians as a breed and he didn't care a hoot about ideological consistency. Thus he loved Robert Stanfield and Dalton Camp but not Mr. Camp's admiree, Richard Nixon. He got along splendidly with Peter Reilly, Pauline Jewett and John Diefenbaker. He laughed at Mel Watkins's one-liners as heartily as he did at those of Sophie, Stephen and, on rare occasions, at those of David too. He loved Lester Pearson with a passion and under his armpit was tattooed the motto, "Neither a Trudeaumaniac nor a Trudeauphobe be, for then you will see what's there to be seen."

The Jaded Observer had first met Trudeau in 1964 when they had fought the good fight together as interviewers in the good old Seven Days. Trudeau had gone on to better things, but he and the Jaded Observer stayed in touch. Most of their later colloquies were in public, some in private.

The Jaded Observer vacillated in his view of Trudeau. In 1968 he didn't like Trudeau's radical chicci friends; in 1972 he didn't like Trudeau's radical chicci enemies. But then he asked himself: Are prime ministers on constant public display really any more free to pick their friends and enemies than Jaded Observers on constant public display? The varied answers the Jaded Observer gave himself to that question were workable but not always comfortable.

One of the Jaded Observer's best friends in Ottawa was a Trudeaucrat, an Irish Catholic by background and thus a natural Hegelian. The Friendly Trudeaucrat was a slum-reared, bootstrap-raised, Oxford-trained technocrat who sincerely believed that ideas, planning and techniques could really solve problems. He was as thin, precise and decisive as the Jaded Observer was fat, sloppy and ditherish.

The Friendly Trudeaucrat, unlike the Jaded Observer, did not believe in the cult of the political personality. Although he had been with Trudeau from the very beginning, it was because of Trudeau's ideas and character, rather than out of opportunism or the pull of Trudeau charisma. He was one of the kindest and most decent men the Jaded Observer had met in Ottawa and one who gave freely and happily of his time and of his day. The Jaded Observer really liked the Trudeaucrat, although he felt, perhaps wrongly, that his friend hadn't prowled as many political back alleys as had he.

Neither the Friendly Trudeaucrat nor the Jaded Observer joined the Trudeau Odyssey that fall of 1972. The Trudeaucrat, a very close aide of Trudeau-Ulysses, stayed home. Each night, Penelope-style, he ravelled and unravelled the tangles of the campaign web spun by Trudeau. The Jaded Observer too stayed at home, watching the campaign from the vantage point of the Hill and the comfort of his living-room TV set.

Now the Jaded Observer had a problem which only his friend could solve. The Jaded Observer, with neither spirit nor flesh willing, was asked by his superiors to pick a leader to cover on election night. The Jaded Observer wanted an obvious winner, one preferably close to home, a client with the big votes and the big bucks who would make election night a happy, profitable, pleasure-ridden romp.

The Jaded Observer spoke to his friend and got what seemed at the time to be some very good tips. "The press is really making a mistake on this one," the Trudeaucrat said. "Trudeau will come back bigger and better than ever before."

Here was a clue to the answer he sought. Then, in the midst of an extraordinarily quiet election campaign, the Jaded Observer had a conversation with a dispirited Doug Fisher. He was told by the big pundit-out (a man whom the Jaded Observer had in the past not liked but whom he now regarded with a respect and affection that bordered on the rapturous) that Trudeau was going to win big—160 seats or better.

To the Jaded Observer, trained at his father's knee that right and wrong were dialectically pre-determined, it seemed that if the Thesis Trudeaucrat and the Antithesis Pundit had arrived at the same electoral synthesis, who was he to quarrel with the Fates? The happy Jaded Observer immediately informed his superiors that Prime Minister Trudeau was his choice for client on election night.

In a later colloquy, the Friendly Trudeaucrat explained to the Jaded Observer that what the country was voting for was the best manager and the best management team. This the Trudeau Lyceum had proven it was for the past four years. Plaza politics and charisma were out. The prime minister was four years older, more settled down and wiser, and so was the country. In 1968, said his friend to the Jaded Observer, Trudeau could only hint at his administrative talents and abilities. In four years he had demonstrably proven them.

Willy-nilly the Jaded Observer was becoming immersed in the Lyceum think-tank and was enjoying the walking on the waters. He was rapidly forgetting the lessons he had learned in the back alleys of the Press Gallery that he had been prowling the previous two years. He was in heady, higher-class company now and was more than willing to forget the foul-smelling dung heaps of his former paparazzi days.

Several weeks before the campaign came to a close, he was rudely awakened from his blissful reveries by a bandit friend, one Vic Mackie, whose instincts and judgements the Jaded Observer had always trusted. The bandit Mackie, whose contacts in the Prairies were of a vintage that even pre-dated the birth of the Jaded Observer, informed the latter that the Prairies were a Liberal drought. Trudeau, he said, would be lucky if he held on to three of the eleven Prairie seats he carried in 1968.

The Jaded Observer was alarmed. He now remembered a previous colloquy with his friend shortly after Barrett's BC victory, when he, the Jaded Observer, had argued this could only help the NDP and hurt the Liberals in the next federal election. He was told by the Friendly Trudeaucrat, presumably acting on BC regional desk input, that there was no correlation between provincial and federal voting patterns.

"How are the Liberals doing in BC?" the Jaded Observer asked the bandit.

"That's strictly a two-way race—the NDP and the Tories," the bandit Mackie replied.

A Liberal drought on the Prairies and in Lotusland raised the inevitable question: Was Stanfield country shrinkable? This the bandit Mackie could not answer. But the Jaded Observer knew where to go to find out. Dalton Camp and his Maritime Liberal equivalent, Ned Beliveau, pronounced the Maritimes a 1968 repeat performance, with the Liberals perhaps picking up two or three seats. Quebec contacts in Liberal party circles were telling the Observer that the Créditistes were alive and well and not hiding in Argentina. Dalton Camp and lifelong Toronto Liberal and NDP politicos, who were the Observer's friends, were now telling him that the Golden Horseshoe was acting up and was any party's for the pitching.

The Jaded Observer reported the bad news he had seen and heard to his friend, the Trudeaucrat. The Trudeaucrat had his answers. Never mind, he said; the Tories are traditionally a rural party, the Liberals an urban party. The Jaded Observer found that hard to believe since, even in the débâcle of 1968, Stanfield had taken the cities of St. John's, Charlottetown, Halifax, Fredericton, Moncton and St. John, and out West had carried three of the four Edmonton seats and two of the three Calgary seats (the latter two cities being the fastest growing in the country).

His friend's observation also flew in the face of history, Tory Toronto being something even the Jaded Observer had encountered in full growth. Besides, if Davis could sweep Toronto in 1971, couldn't the Big Blue Machine do something for its old Stanfield pal and ally in October 1972?

As for Ottawa, it had always been Liberal and would remain so, the Trudeaucrat thought. Nor did he think much of the NDP. The "corporate welfare bum" charge was dumb, the Trudeaucrat said, for any Canadian knew the more the corporations were taxed the more they passed on the tax burden to the consumers in the form of higher prices. But, if that were true, the Jaded Observer wondered quietly to himself, wouldn't it be best not to tax the corporations at all?

That, he knew, would be the riposte that Lewis would offer to any Trudeauite or Turnerite who would dare to debate the subject with him in the labour beer halls and country curling rinks that Lewis performed in best. The Jaded Observer, who had prowled those beer halls and country curling rinks for years, knew that Joe Lunchpail and the Farmer and his Frau were listening and applauding as little David told them that if they paid their taxes, the companies and company executives who lived off their sweat and labour should pay theirs too.

The Jaded Observer remembered a conversation long ago in Trudeau charisma days when his friend explained that the Lyceum approach was to divide problems into two areas: economic-material and psychic-spiritual. Both areas had been given a lot of think-tank thought. It had been decided in the Lyceum that in the time-frame of the seventies and coming eighties, it would be best to be conservative in the economic-material area and liberal, perhaps even radical, in the psychic-spiritual area. This accounted, said the Friendly Trudeaucrat, for the de-emphasis on King-Pearson welfare legislation and certainly a curtailment of any Walter Gordonish attempts to buy back Canada. This accounted, too, for Trudeau's psychic-spiritual emphasis on federalism, on Opportunities for Youth, on genetic engineering, on the Leisure

Society and the other future-shock problems that technology on the march would inevitably bring.

The Jaded Observer remembered that in that ancient colloquy he had declared himself, if given the choice, to be a liberal-radical in the economic-material area and perhaps a bit conservative in the psychic-spiritual. Reflecting on these two categories in the fall of 1972, the Jaded Observer recognized that the two areas were not watertight compartments, foreign ownership seeming to many far more spiritual-psychic than economic-material.

In the fall of 1972, the Jaded Observer recognized too that for those stung by unemployment and inflation, the money spent by the Trudeau government in the spiritual-psychic area was bitterly resented. Those receiving the benefits from the new Spiritual-Psychic Order were middle- and upper-middle-class participants in a revolution of rising expectations. Like all revolutionaries, they were yelling: Too little and too late! To the Jaded Observer, watching the Liberals in the last weeks of October 1972 being simultaneously attacked from the top floors and the basement of the vertical mosaic, there seemed little point in continuing the colloquy with the Trudeaucrat.

The electronic anteater now clearly sniffed a ghastly Trudeau defeat in Anglophonia. Rapid phone calls across the country to Liberal-Tory-NDP politicos in the final week only confirmed his worst suspicions. The by-now very unhappy Jaded Observer knew that Trudeau, his client, no longer had the big votes and the big bucks. Election night with him would not be a happy, profitable, pleasure-ridden romp.

Indeed, what the Jaded Observer foresaw was a Berlin-Bunkerish election night, the Trudeau client unreachable, his aides in total disarray and the atmosphere tense . . . tense . . . tense. He therefore contacted his superiors and told them of the election-night disaster coming ahead. Pleading that he was too old and too weak to be master of ceremonies at a Gotterdammerung, he asked for younger blood to take his place.

His superiors thought the Jaded Observer excessively alarmist and insisted he man his post. Willing or not, the Jaded Observer would be a clinging wallflower at Liberal headquarters at Ottawa's Skyline Hotel on election night, 1972.

Chapter Thirteen
Message Received:
The Folding of the Universe and Lessons Learned

The election-night scene at Liberal headquarters in the Skyline Hotel was as bad as anything the Jaded Observer had foreseen. As he arrived he was informed that all cameras and reporters had been barred from direct access to the headquarters of the prime minister, his aides and party officials. Unlike the cameras present in the Halifax headquarters of Robert Lazarus and his cheering faithful, and unlike, too, the cameras present in the Toronto lair of Lewis and his cheering faithful, the camera in Trudeau-land was present only in a press room filled exclusively with reporters with nothing to do except watch TV on a set the Skyline Hotel had kindly provided for the occasion.

Many of the reporters present (particularly banditi Vic Mackie and Arthur Blakeley) had received the message early. They were not impressed with the gain of three Liberal seats in the Maritimes. On the TV screens they were watching early returns showing the Tories and NDP leading in many Toronto seats, omens that they had been warned meant an Ontario Trudeau disaster, with far less seats there than Pearson had thrice taken.

At that moment the peasant paps were informed that the prime minister was arriving at the front door of the Skyline Hotel. It was to be the first of his only two meetings with the press that night.

To the paps and illuminati who had done their homework, it was obvious that the prime minister had, as yet, *not* received the message. Beaming at his new-found penetration in the Maritimes, he and his Mountie entourage brushed their way through the paparazzi jungle of mikes and pencils awaiting him. One wierd question from a jaded aging paparazznik did get through: "Is that flower you're wearing the colour of blood?" the old pap asked about the red carnation in the PM's lapel. "No, it's the colour of the Liberal Party," said the surprised prime minister, as he entered the Skyline elevator for the fifteenth floor Liberal party retreat.

What did the silly old pap mean, Trudeau must have wondered. Was he Dracula sucking the blood of his Lewis-Stanfield victims? Or was *he* the *victim* being rapidly drained of the political lifeblood of majority government? As for the silly old pap, he meant no disrespect. He was merely a rabbinical student, asking his rabbi a question he hoped would bring the rabbi gently out of the clouds (where he'd been flying with the Almighty) to land, hopefully softly, on the rough ground awaiting below.

The disciple didn't see the rabbi the rest of the evening, although he did make the odd unsuccessful try at contact. Donning his harlequin costume, he tensely did his "Dance, clown, dance" routine that evening for the eyes and ears of the reporters assembled around him and also for the eyes and ears of Anglophonia whenever his superiors chose to call on his peculiar talents.

But his mind was really on the Dance of the Dialectic that night. Would Trudeau discover that in the cruelest pirouette of that peculiar dance, his Lyceum was now and really had been for some time the Cave of Darkness? What would he say once he burst out into the dazzling sunlight?

As the witching hour approached, and no one really knew who was actually going to get the most seats—

Robert Lazarus or Toppling Trudeau—the press, growing
tense, relieved themselves in a bandinage of one-liners.
"The poor bastard's going to have to go from philosopher-
king to Mackenzie King—and he's got less than an hour
to do it," said one jaded silly old pap, more in sorrow
than in petty. "The land is strong, but the people are
wrong," said a former Liberal advertising apparatchik,
now just a grubby paparazznik like the rest of us.

Finally the prime minister himself appeared and, de-
clining the dialectic of an encounter with the electronic-
print ants that had finally ruined his picnic, he issued a
short statement. "The universe is unfolding as it should,"
he said, fully indicating that the first lesson he had learned
was that shadows flickering by on the walls of caves are
neither real nor just. He had finally learned that he had
danced his Last Tango with the Dialectic in his role as
philosopher-king. The Lyceum and the Cave of Darkness
would soon be put to the torch and to the wreckers of
Cohen and Cohen and Public Works.

Still, like all who emerge suddenly from the Cave of
Darkness to face the dazzling sunlight, there is the sudden
shock of stars in your eyes. In the subsequent dizziness,
the odd mistake can be made.

The Jaded Observer, for one, wondered at first whether
the message had really been received. Was the universe
"unfolding as it should" one more stubborn intellectual
holding-action by a tired philosopher? Or did it indicate
that the Hegelian was becoming a historical materialist,
ready and willing to take all the necessary hardships and
joys that come with those first rude shocks of being forci-
bly stood on one's own head?

The Jaded Observer would have preferred the prime
minister to say: "My universe is folding, as it should."
For in astronomy, the world is Copernican—the earth and
its earthlings revolve around the sun. In politics the world
is Ptolemaic—Sun Kings who wish to hang on to their

thrones must learn to revolve around earth and earthlings.

The Jaded Observer wondered still more when he later heard rumours that Trudeau and his Quebec followers took their rejection by Anglophonia to be a racist, bigoted rejection of the new Trudeau meritocracy. There were rumours that he and some of his top Quebec people were going to pack it in, thus surely packing the country in in the process. The Jaded Observer's wonder took on the proportions of alarm when he heard Liberal talk of Rosedale "rednecks" and listened to the prime minister in a Throne Speech debate harangue the Tories as if Stanfield were a Gauleiter with a following of 106 storm troopers.

The only "rednecks" in Rosedale the Jaded Observer had ever met were Trinity graduates (their children enrolled in the Toronto French School) who had burned themselves badly during a winter holiday in the Bahamas. Indeed, many of these "rednecks" bore a striking resemblance to the Oxford-donnish members of the Canadian National Liberation Front he had met at so many political conventions. (The Gallup Poll was later to show that the "redneck" vote of the upper-middle classes dropped sharply for the Liberals, stayed steady for the Tories and rose, wonder of wonders, eleven percentage points for the NDP.)

The Jaded Observer also knew that the teeming, huddled masses of the Golden Horseshoe couldn't care less if Ottawa's civil service was entirely Zambian, let alone bilingual or unilingual Francophone. They were interested in bread and butter and not the Lyceum Circus on the Rideau.

Bigots the Jaded Observer had met many times. He'd seen them, alas, in all parties. Alack, in the Press Gallery too. He'd seen them rally to Trudeau's One Canada and to Trudeau's handling of the October Crisis. And he'd met some who'd rather vote for Lewis, the Jew, than

Trudeau, the Francophone. (In 1966, the Jaded Observer had worked for the Democratic party in the state of Pennsylvania. There his bosses, Larry O'Brien and Joe Napolitan, showed him surveys that proved Pennsylvanians rated Jews just below Unitarians and far higher than Catholics as suitable material for the office of governor.)

The 29th Parliament had its share of bigots, but in all parties there were bright, new young faces. The Jaded Observer could agree with Dief, the thirty-three-year veteran of Parliament, that if the 29th Parliament was not Trudeau's Finest Hour, the members of it were the Brightest and the Best in thirty-three years.

What particularly saddened the Jaded Observer about the behaviour brought about by the Trudeau sunstroke, was that the Francophone members of the post-October cabinet—Trudeau, Pelletier, Marchand, Lalonde, Chrétien and Ouellette—were the best array of Francophone talent assembled anywhere in the country and the Brightest and the Best Francophone assemblage in the country's history. They understood Francophonia very well but their vision of Anglophonia was not quite 20-20.

For example, the Jaded Observer didn't quite think that the PM's later "after Austerlitz" aphorism re future successes in future elections was quite apt. After Austerlitz, a historian informed the Jaded Observer, there was Tilsit and then the march on Moscow, Elba exile, return and Waterloo. Perhaps a look-out from the East Block on to a street called Wellington would have brought a more appropriate metaphor for the eyes and ears of Anglophonia. Anglophones don't like Caesar (he conquered Britain) and they don't like Napoleon (he killed Lord Nelson).

Still, the sunstroke was only temporary and quite natural for a recent refugee from a Cave of Darkness. The Hegelian had become a historical materialist, for

Trudeau announced that he was holding on to power and said he was willing to "learn the lessons of October 30."

(Hegelians don't learn lessons, they teach them. Their syntheses are a priori. Historical materialists never teach lessons [or shouldn't]; they learn them. Their conclusions are posteriori and are often rudely enforced by the most sobering teacher of all: the swift kicks in the posterior that life repeated gives to those who dare to poke their rears into areas they don't belong.)

What lessons had Trudeau learned? From Mackenzie King he was learning that you're less likely to get politically fucked using crystal balls than real balls and that the message of the medium is often more accurate than the emperor's messenger. From Mackenzie King he also learned that material realities demand both a house-cleaning and a Godfatherly loyalty to those who have served, if not always wisely, at least always faithfully.

The Oxford dons of Athenian democracy—Ivan Head, Peter Roberts, Jim Davey—were replaced by the Neapolitan dons of the Ontario Liberal mafia—Martin O'Connell, Torrence Wylie, John Roberts—but the Oxford dons were given other useful assignments to perform for the Godfather in the new treacherous minority waters. From Mackenzie King and Lester Pearson Trudeau had also learned that politics is the art of the possible, not Mission Impossible.

(The new program secretary, John Roberts, was once asked by the Jaded Observer, "What's your time-frame for decision-making?" "My time-frame is today," replied the jaunty new Neapolitan, Oxford-trained Don. The only critical-path flow chart that hung on his wall was a calendar.)

From Mackenzie King Trudeau learned that if the key to holding power was an adroit swing to the left, so be it. For Mackenzie King had always provided the greatest magic elixir for any leader to swallow and survive, the elixir of "Let Parliament Decide." Trudeau, who had scorned Parliament as a waste of time, inhabited by a pack of "nobodies," was to learn quickly that, if properly used, Parliament could be more than a sanctuary. It could become an impregnable fortress.

But Trudeau was really not quite going from philosopher-king to Mackenzie King. That old harlequin had never had a power base of his own. He relied on Mackenzie for BC, Gardiner for the Prairies, Howe and Rogers for Ontario, Lapointe for Quebec and Angus L. for the Maritimes.

Trudeau was like Laurier: he had a base of his own. If toppled in Anglophonia, Trudeau was still king of Francophonia. Like Laurier, too, Trudeau had his own following in Anglophonia, not quite as devoted as the Anglophone followers that went down with Laurier in flames in 1917, but a following prepared to go one hell of a distance, if only he'd meet them half way.

The 38.46% of the vote Trudeau got was not *all* Francophone. Unlike Mackenzie King, whom nobody really hated and nobody really liked, Trudeau was a man whom people either hated or liked. Trudeau picked up or dropped his own marbles. King spent his lifetime in power watching others fall to pieces. There was more dignity and pride in the Trudeau approach. While it was politically risky, he'd continue it, determined to make those who hated him in October 1972 at least like him in June 1974.

The Jaded Observer's election-night remark about philosopher-king to Mackenzie King was really, after all, only superficial. Sure 1972 looked like 1925. Trudeau was seemingly clinging to power with the help of the NDP, as King had done with the Farmer-Progressives and the two Labour MPs (Woodsworth, the Methodist, and Heaps, the Hebrew). Eugene Forsey was around then, as he was now, to act as the constitutional master of ceremonies, and Lewis the Hebrew and his bench-mate

Tommy the Baptist sure bore an uncanny resemblance to the twin Socialist dynamos of 1925.

But the resemblance was really superficial, as superficial as the post-election-night argument of punditi-out James Eayrs that Trudeau had no right to stay in office, even though he had 3½ percentage points more than Stanfield in a One Canada in which all voters, be they Francophone or Anglophone, are supposedly equal.

Trudeau had every right to remain in office and take his chances as Lewis had every right to keep him in office and take his chances. Indeed, there was more to be learned from St. Laurent and 1957 than both men cared openly to admit.

St. Laurent had proven Laurier wrong on two counts. He had proven that another French-Canadian could be prime minister, could win two smashing victories and, when defeated, could retire gracefully because he was beaten by a newer and more vital man with newer and more progressive ideas; and *not* beaten simply because he was a French Canadian. Trudeau's "mea culpa" vulnerable image that slowly began to emerge after October owed more to a growing understanding of the value of St. Laurent's modesty, simplicity and good grace than it owed to a slowly, very slowly growing appreciation of Pearson's self-deprecating talents.

From St. Laurent, there was also this important tacit lesson to be learned. No single man, no single party *was* and *is* indispensible to Canada. The land was strong; it could and would survive a minority government; it could and would survive in a Stanfield government, should that necessity arise.

That 1957 lesson David Lewis had learned well. A close Lewis aide told the Jaded Observer shortly after the election that had the NDP backed Stanfield rather than Trudeau, there would have been a snap session, a snap election and 1958 all over again (at least for the NDP). The Lewis

forces did not scoff at Robert Lazarus. They knew him
to be the formidable Incredible Canadian he really was.
They knew because they had done battle with him in their
four provincial strongholds and watched him whomp them
in Ontario and Manitoba, beat them narrowly in Saskatchewan and come within an inch in their newly acquired
BC turf.

There were still some in Trudeau's closest circles who,
for bizarre reasons of their own, seemed to think Stanfield
was the new, post-October Trudeau's best asset. The new
Trudeau, however, had learned his lessons well. He knew
that Stanfield would not die nor slowly fade away; nor
would he be done in as was The Chief. There were now
two long-distance runners in the race, Robert Lazarus and
Toppled Trudeau. The winner of that marathon affair
would reign long, maybe as long as Mackenzie King.

That the new marathon race for the Mackenzie King
Cup was strictly a two-man affair was the key lesson to
be learned by everyone in the political schoolhouse that
was Ottawa in 1973. No one knew the lesson better than
David Lewis, who had learned and taught many a lesson
before.

In the common-law marriage of convenience with Trudeau, Lewis, alas, was the spouse, lacking legitimate
status for either himself or the offspring of the marriage.
Morally, he could claim all the credit for the *good* Trudeau
legislation of 1973, but legally they bore the Trudeau
government stamp. On the hustings the Trudeau forces
could and would take credit for them.

Lalonde's universal Family Allowance plan no doubt
owed much to Lewis's hidden and not so hidden per-
suaders, but the impoverished large families of Quebec
and the Maritimes would have no way of knowing that.
Nor, for that matter, would the middle-income families
of urban Canada remember for long either the anger they
had felt at the deprivations of FISP, or that the credit for

the new Lalonde plan was really due to David.

The tougher foreign-investment bill owed much to the NDP clout but the "Down Periscope!" message was loud and clear in Honderich-Gordon-Toronto *Star* land. That submarine would prowl the waters for the Liberals in the next election, for Trudeau was no longer playing Canada's Generalissimo Ky to the Canadian National Liberation Front.

Nor could David really run another corporate-welfare-bum campaign because neither Trudeau nor Stanfield would let him. The compromise arranged on the subject in 1973 and the monitoring device built into that compromise would let both the Tories and the Liberals off the hook next March, should the corporations fail to deliver the promised jobs the tax cuts were supposed to create.

Even the tougher Election Expenses Bill, in the wake of Watergate, did little for the NDP and a lot for Trudeau. Watergate Nixon could no longer shed reflected lustre on Lazarus Bob; nor did Watergate Nixon have the time and energy to play Nixonomics. Watergate Nixon was a paper tiger and Anglophonia could now bask in anti-American glory and reflect on how much better *our* Chairman was than *theirs*.

Even in the NDP strongholds in the West, David had to watch helplessly as Trudeau got at least a minimum of second-billing in the Queen's tour of the West and in the conference with the Western premiers. Second billing is better than no billing at all. If the Queen's Visit and the Western Conference didn't really help Trudeau, it also didn't, in the immortal phrase of the Jewish Catskill comedian, "really hurt him either." Nor for that matter did the world-wide spotlight of the first Commonwealth Conference (Queen Elizabeth et al) ever held on Canadian soil.

But what was most frightening of all for the NDP was

that David Lewis had proved what neither Woodsworth, Coldwell nor Douglas before him were either willing or able to do, namely, that there *is* a difference between the two old-line parties. If, as the Jaded Observer had once said, Liberals Trudeau, Marchand and Pelletier were really "socialists in a hurry," it would be fair to say that the Lewis balance-of-power forces were acting as "Liberals in a hurry," as St. Laurent had once predicted they would.

The ferocity with which Lewis attacked "the power-hungry" Stanfield wouldn't play in either Peoria or Lilac. Anglophonia knew Robert Lazarus to be honest, patient, kind and considerate and the fierceness of the attacks upon him only made Anglophones wonder about David. The gallery peasant paps constantly twitted Lewis about being Trudeau's "pet" bird in a gilded cage. Lewis's occasional angry outburst at them for their failure to understand the subtleties of his position only reminded them of the bad old arrogant Trudeau of yore. The paps could see no *real* difference in the two positions of Trudeau and Lewis.

Nor, for that matter, could the Underhill socialists who had once embraced Woodsworth and, rejecting what they felt was the labour-dominated NDP, had then reserved their affections for L.B. Pearson and P.E. Trudeau. Men like King Gordon-Graham Spry-Frank Scott-Michael Oliver began to wonder, if not aloud, at least to themselves, whether the glories of a Hartzian-Horowitz-fragment socialism were really worth it when the Ramadan Feasts of a Canadian NDP-Liberal New Deal coalition were staring them in the face. (The Jaded Observer began to wonder about future Ramadan Feasts when, looking up from his wine glass one wintry evening in the parliamentary restaurant, he noticed King Gordon, Michael Oliver, Marc Lalonde and P.E. Trudeau enjoying the gay camaraderie of Rideau Bedouins in the night.)

By the summer of 1973 reporters were telling tales of

a rebellion in the NDP "crack" research team and colum-
nists were either writing about the Lewis search for a
"divorce" or the NDP as a third "old-line party." The
conscience-of-the-nation role for the NDP was going fast
and political dividends for the future were few and far
between. In the next election Lewis would have to depend
for survival on the tough nitty-gritty door-to-door canvass-
ing of yore and a lot of help from his friends, Barrett,
Blakeney and Schreyer.

In that next election, Lewis would be facing a Stanfield
as resilient and tough as ever and a new post-October
Trudeau who was learning the finer points of political
gamesmanship he didn't have to know in charisma days
and didn't bother to learn in the Lyceum. Now Trudeau
was mastering them at an astonishing pace.

The bilingualism debate in the spring of 1973 was politics at its most brutal, but it had nailed Quebec down
for the immediate moment, opened up old Tory wounds
and would enable Liberals to spend their organizing
energies in Ontario and the West. After this debate, the
Stanfield Tory energies would have to be diverted and
devoted to closing the wounds, making slow and painful
inroads into the even more solid Quebec citadel while
at the same time getting little help from their provincial
friends, energy-taxing Lougheed and Hydrogate Davis.

The new Trudeau was now also learning a lesson that
Pearson and Stanfield had long mastered before him, the
difference between wit and humour. Wit is directed at
someone else's expense, humour at your own. But the
latter draws double the laughs (your own and your audience) and who knows, in the long run, maybe double
the votes. The new eager-to-learn-politics Trudeau was,
wonder of wonders, even learning, albeit a bit awkwardly,
to tell jokes on himself.

For the Press Gallery dinner of 1973, a request went
out from the PM's new press secretary, Pierre O'Neill,

to the Jaded Observer. (That harlequin was now doing, among other things, a weekly radio satire-gossip bit, playing Abie's Nose to the Wild Irish Rose of his beloved comrade-in-arms Patrick MacFadden.) Would the Jaded Observer care to contribute his, by now legendary, satirical talents to the prime minister's gallery dinner speech, as he had so splendidly done for Pierre O'Neill's Press Gallery president's speech two years ago? The Jaded Observer, thrilled at the opportunity to joust anonymously with his old Winnipeg college classmate, Whipper Billy Grogan (the Stanfield jokesmith) agreed, provided the motif for the Trudeau speech was humour, not the dimless wit that Trudeau had employed with such futility at these gatherings before.

The conditions of the Jaded Observer were met. At the 1973 Press Gallery dinner, an astonished Trudeau found that, for the first time in five years, jokes delivered at his own expense were getting him the laughs and almost the affection that for years now had always been Stanfield's. It was a new experience for Trudeau and, as he later told the Jaded Observer, an enjoyable one. (Although he did blanch when the Jaded Observer noted sadly that the PM's poor timing had ruined some of the Jaded Observer's more minor comic masterpieces.)

The new Trudeau's attitude to the gallery (to both its illuminati and its paparazzi divisions) had also changed as theirs had changed vis-à-vis him. Their revolution was over and done with. They had fed hemlock to Trudeau's philosopher-king image, guillotined his Robespierre and Marie Antoinette disguises, taken an axe to his Carry Nation notions and Viet-Conged the Generalissimo· Ky's to the Peaceable Kingdom. But in the process they had really done him a favour. The gallery, after all, was Anglophonia in miniature. Its members were from all floors of the vertical mosaic and from all parts of ·the country. They belonged to everything from Women's Lib to the Canadian National Liberation Front and from Kiwanis to the Knights of Columbus. If he couldn't handle them, maybe Trudeau really couldn't handle Anglo-phonia.

The gallery treated the post-October Trudeau with a new kind of detached neutrality. Trudeau walked through the government lobbies after Question Period and hardly a paparazznik or a pundit even looked his way.

But the old animosity was gone. They and the Anglo-phonia they reported to had humbled him. Trudeau was no longer the smug, perfect little boy who had everything he wanted and to whom everything came effortlessly, the perfect little boy everybody admired but secretly hated and envied, the perfect little boy that M. Charles Cohen had so devastatingly satirized in a nationally syndicated feature article some years ago.

Trudeau had been to the top of the mountain, had been pushed off but had miraculously risen to fight again. Now he was like many a gallery member who, in his stupor, drunken or otherwise, had fallen off or been pushed off many a mountain top in his day.

It now seemed to the Jaded Observer and others that Trudeau had learned from Pearson probably the most valu-able lesson of all, that the comic opera of Neapolitan poli-tics, while not as intellectually productive as the colloquy of Athens on the Rideau, was a hell of a lot more fun. Trudeau was now learning to take in his stride the Yoga-class Ostry-Haidasz "leaks," Dief's prison dogs, the Millhaven Cookbook of Harold Ballard and the crystal balls of the mysterious gypsies.

The gallery was naturally overjoyed to see the return of Italian politics to the Hill and noted that a determined Trudeau Godfather looked like he could not only cope with it but enjoy it. It was also nice for Charlie Lynch, Doug Fisher and the other punditi-out to know that maybe now their readership in the Prime Minister's Office had gone beyond the file clerk's desk.

In any event, as the punditi-in and punditi-out, the radical chicci, the banditi, the paparazzi and the Canadian National Liberation Front watched the flames rising higher and higher from the Lyceum Cave of Darkness Trudeau had put the torch to, and as they listened to the crackling sounds of burning regional desks and critical-path flow charts, they must have wondered what kind of steel-tempered and better-tempered new Trudeau would ultimately emerge from the ashes of the old. Watching and wondering too, the Jaded Observer noted, were Turner, the heir-apparent and the now all-too-obvious hare-apparent, and right behind him, coming on strong and tooting away, the new, irrepressible Road Runner, Marc Lalonde. Watching and wondering too was Anglophonia, whose final decision on Trudeau, Stanfield and Lewis had yet to be made.

And, smiling behind them all, was the wicked and wily Dialectic Dancer, eagerly waiting in the wings to step once more on to the marathon dance floor to make sweet mincemeat out of the Trudeau-Stanfield-Lewis concoction she had served up to the Canadian people on October 30th last.

Epilogue

Enough Is Enough!

Well, my readers, we've come a long way since you last saw me bouncing on my father's knee in the childhood of my Winnipeg days. In those days, when the arguments between my father and Leibel Basman, the Bolshevik philosopher-king of our neighbourhood, became too heated and violence threatened to ensue, my mother (a close personal friend of the Jaded Observer, by the way) would bring instant peace by invoking the ancient war cry of the females of her "stem" tribe: "Genug iz genug!" (or as Mr. Barrett so succinctly put it to the electors of BC: "Enough is enough!")

Still, it's my epic and I've got a few things left to say. What my father and Leibel Basman quarrelled most bitterly over was the Permanence of the Dance of the Dialectic. Did the dance come to a clean stop in the Utopia of a classless society, Jewish or otherwise, or did it simply go on and on, forever and forever spinning antitheses to the theses that sprung forth from its syntheses?

For both men, Leibel Basman, the Bolshevik philosopher-king, and Yoshua Falk Zolf, the Jewish nationalist philosopher-king, the last answer to the eternal question was unthinkable. Both men wanted the peace and permanence that all philosopher-kings by conviction and temperament desire. For Leibel Basman, the dance would end in the permanence of a classless Communist Utopia; for my father, the dance would end in the perma-

111

nence of a classless Zionist Utopia.

But I, the son of one and the admirer of the other, am neither Communist nor Jewish nationalist. (A Canadian subject I was born; a Canadian subject I hope to die.) Unlike Trudeau, the recent convert, I've *always* been a humble historical materialist, convinced by repeated swift kicks in my posteriori conclusions that the manoeuvres, postures, pratfalls and tours de force of the Dialectic are endless.

What they hold in store for the Jaded Observer I do not know. He, quite frankly, needs all the luck he can get. So good luck to you, Jaded Observer: may you outlive your enemies who are legion and continue bringing joy to the few stray clients who still come up and see you sometime.

Farewell banditi, punditi, paparazzi; farewell Trudeau-Stanfield-Lewis! To you all I bequeath the House on Parliament Hill. This punchy fiddler is getting off the Peace Tower roof before he's carilloned to death. But worry not; I'll be OK. I've got this great new job: I'm the lead in the CBC's first multi-cultural epic—an all-Jewish version of *Jesus Christ Superstar*!!

("O Dialectic! O Dialectic! Have you no sense of shame?"

"No, schmuck—and don't you ever forget it!!")

Glossary

The Parliamentary Press Gallery and those journalistic academics who spend much of their working hours and most of their sober energies on the reporting and analyzing of federal affairs in Ottawa are those ladies and gentlemen and just plain persons who played the media New Romans to the Trudeau Greeks in the Trudeau Lyceum years, June 1968 to October 30, 1972.

This particular collection of great Canadians can be divided on a class-structure basis into two basic classifications: the illuminati and the paparazzi.

The illuminati are the Brightest and the Best, the aristocrat class of the media New Romans. Its Press Gallery branch members, as a rule, are distinguished educationally with a minimum of a BA or a Bachelor of Journalism; if not, a highschool diploma, training in Pitman shorthand, fast typing plus an ability to adopt the manners and mores of one's betters will do.

Academic brilliance in the gallery's illuminati branch is not a necessity; indeed, for the most sensitive, frail types, it can provoke the handicap of being branded "witty" or "eccentric." The illuminati should write and speak soberly and earnestly as if they mean every word they write and as if every word they write and speak has meaning.

The illuminati are, by definition, to be taken seriously, if not by the Canadian public, at least by the politicians.

If this healthy awe and respect is not automatically forth-coming, the illuminati will exercise the alternative option of taking *themselves* seriously. If the former option does materialize the illuminati may still exercise the latter option, and frequently do.

All illuminati, by definition, have either a newspaper column, an on-air credit, at the very least a by-line and many have all three. (Some illuminati, of course, have none of these but are spoken of in the gallery in hushed tones.)

The illuminati, as used in this heroic epic, is a collective blanket term embracing all the members of four distinct sub-species: the punditi-in, the punditi-out, the radical chicci and the banditi. As a blanket term, illuminati has an Occham's razor's edge—it does not embrace the lower class of the media New Romans, the peasant paparazzi. Thus, all illuminati are either punditi-in, punditi-out, radical chicci or banditi . . . or vice-versa.

PUNDITI-IN: Those members of the illuminati who, in their columns, books, broadcasts, op-ed Newthink pieces and feature stories, were generally speaking favourable to the Trudeau administration in both its Athenian phase and the deluge aftermath. Their requests for prime ministerial interviews, aphorisms and decantations were (and perhaps still are) always automatically placed in the punditi-in basket in the Prime Minister's Office (PMO).

The puntiti-in contain a very small number of college professors and a fair number of former Canadian university newspaper editors and star reporters. Experience in Fleet Street journalism is an automatic admission ticket; actual physical contact with Lord Beaverbrook himself allows you to bring in a close friend for almost nothing. The punditi-in are invariably male, never fat and do not possess a funny last name, nor a sense of humour.

PUNDITI-OUT: Those members of the illuminati who, in their columns, books, broadcasts, op-ed Thinkpieces and feature stories, were, generally speaking, unfavourable to the Trudeau administration in both its Athenian phase and the deluge aftermath.

Punditi-out are not invariably male (witness Montreal economist Dian Cohen, who is definitely *not* invariably male), are sometimes fat (witness the shocking obesity of Charles Lynch, Douglas Fisher, Professor James Eayrs, Walter Stewart and George Bain) and do possess funny last names (witness Lubor Zink and James Eayrs). Punditi-out always have a sense of humour (witness Lubor Zink and James Eayrs). Punditi-out rarely request Trudeau interviews, aphorisms and declamations. If they do, their requests are usually placed in the punditi-out basket in the PMO.

RADICAL CHICCI: Not an academic in the whole bunch, just a nice bunch of kids insisting on an overview of the Ottawa scene which neither the punditi-in nor the punditi-out were in their view providing.

Close family or marital ties to newspaper proprietors, publishers or just plain old-fashioned rich people are certainly no bar to admission to this fertile sub-species of the illuminati. Failure to toil as an apprentice in the vineyards of small Western and Maritime newspapers is not considered an insuperable barrier to membership; nor is the expert knowledge picked up from on-the-Hill experience of ten or more years an absolute must for admission to the gallery's most exclusive intellectual symposium.

The radical chicci are on intimate terms with the works of Alvin Toffler, Germaine Greer, Lionel Tiger and all bestsellers on the nonfiction list. Early childhood exposure to the Books of Knowledge and the union Encyclopaedia Britannica plus a later judicious college-day skimming of Dr. Adler's Great Books have provided the radical chicci with just enough information about Poverty, Race (particularly blacks and Francophones) and Revolution (particularly Quiet ones) to sustain the proper overview.

Radical chicci, as a rule, skillfully avoid the academic-overkill trap of actual scholarship.

The radical chicci overview can best be described as "socialism if necessary, but not necessarily David Lewis socialism." Noblesse oblige instincts urge them to take a personal hand at the throttle of government but, secretly, they worry that the whole government business might be a bit too easy.

While the radical chicci are invariably young and thin and from good families they do tolerate acolytes who revolve in their orbit, who might be from lesser breeds. These acolytes can also be fat or female or both.

Radical chicci loved the Trudeau of '68 but rejected the October Crisis Trudeau, roughly three months after that event.

Radical chicci, like the punditi-in, always find lunch with senior members of the Privy Council Office an edifying experience. When on television, they smirk a lot and have that self-satisfied dopey look of the inside dopester. The radical chicci are small in numbers but their influence is growing. In ten years they may be the very core of the punditi-in.

THE BANDITI: The ancients of the gallery, some dating back to R.B. Bennett, many to Mackenzie King and all, at least, to St. Laurent. The banditi wouldn't know a Lyceum or a PMO if they fell over it. Not an academic in the whole bunch, just a nice bunch of old-timers, inclined to be conservative, who believe that history tends to repeat itself and when it does it tends to corrupt the thing it repeats absolutely.

THE PAPARAZZI: The peasant class of the Press Gallery and the media New Romans are louts, rascals and high-school drop-outs all. The odd one may have a BA or better but that's usually an aberration. Social breeding and aristocratic connections in this class are well-nigh invisible. The paparazzi are the by-products of audio-visual education and not John Dewey.

The paparazzi class embraces all broadcasters (with the exception of Bruce Phillips, Geoff Scott, Peter Stursberg and Ron Collister), all members of the wire services and all workaday print journalists who print only the facts and just the facts, man. Like termite ants they can eat you up, bit by bit, day by day. The paparazzi are strictly non-U, but always fun to be with. They are the favourites of ministerial executive assistants, broadcast licence owners and newspaper publishers who believe in the theory and practice of objective journalism.